A HANDBOOK ON
HOLY
SPIRIT
BAPTISM

A HANDBOOK ON
HOLY SPIRIT BAPTISM

DON BASHAM

Whitaker House

A HANDBOOK ON HOLY SPIRIT BAPTISM

ISBN-13: 978-0-88368-003-2
ISBN-10: 0-88368-003-3
Printed in the United States of America
© 1969 by Don Basham

Whitaker House
1030 Hunt Valley Circle
New Kensington, PA 15068
www.whitakerhouse.com

22 23 24 25 26 27 28 ᴜᴊ 12 11 10 09 08 07 06

CONTENTS

PART II: *Questions about speaking in tongues*

PART III: *Questions about receiving the baptism in the Holy Spirit*

PREFACE

Today, millions of people have been hearing and sharing the new and exciting news of the 20th Century Pentecost which is sweeping the Christian world. After several years of participating in seminars and conferences here and abroad which dealt with this outpouring of the Holy Spirit, I discovered that every seminar covered much of the same ground and dealt with many of the same primary questions. I also discovered that, while a few books and small pamphlets touched on some of these questions, it seemed that no single volume was available whose primary objective was to answer most of them.

The purpose of A HANDBOOK ON HOLY SPIRIT BAPTISM is to help fill this need. It deals with those primary questions about seeking and receiving the baptism in the Holy Spirit as well as the areas that often block an individual from obtaining this blessing from God. Every question which is included is one that has been asked repeatedly in teaching conferences and seminars over the years. Obviously, most of the areas could have been discussed at much greater length. But bear in mind that this is a handbook, not an encyclopedia.

No claim is made for any new revelation in these pages. Most Spirit-baptized readers will have heard or read about most of the points discussed, although some of the illustrative material may be new.

The book is designed primarily for two groups of Christians: (1) those interested in or seeking to receive the baptism in the Holy Spirit, and (2) those who have already received the baptism and now find themselves with opportunity to minister to others.

While all the material is pertinent, this is not a book which requires reading from beginning to end to be of value. That is why it is called a handbook. Instead of giving titles to the chapters, we have simply allowed the question the chapter deals with to serve as its heading. Then, by checking the table of contents, you can quickly turn to the question of greatest interest or concern to you or to those with whom you may be discussing the subject.

Except for quoted material, the responsibility for the contents of the book is mine. No claim is made for infallibility. Other writers would doubtlessly stress different points and include other material in answering the same questions. A prayerful effort has been made to combine clear Scripture teaching with personal experience, but no "in-depth" study or analysis of Scripture has been attempted. All Scripture references, unless otherwise noted, are from the Revised Standard Version.

Eloquence has been sacrificed on the altar of plain speech, and most of the material is presented in a conversational manner, as in a public meeting. From time to time, I have drawn on the experiences of others. I gratefully acknowledge my indebtedness to them, but most of all to our Lord Jesus Christ, Who is today revealing Himself not only as Savior and Healer, but as Baptizer in the Holy Spirit as well.

PART I

Questions concerning the charismatic movement and the baptism in the Holy Spirit

CHAPTER 1

Some of us who heard of the baptism in the Holy Spirit only recently know practically nothing of its history. Can you give us some background information?

If you are searching for the baptism in the Holy Spirit and the power it promises, the best place to begin is with the New Testament, especially the book of Acts because it describes the ministry of the first group of Spirit-filled believers. Reading the book of Acts, I quickly understood why the Disciples of Christ (the denomination in which I am ordained) originally wanted to be known as a New Testament church and why it proudly claimed a New Testament heritage. It was because the New Testament church was an exciting church, a powerful church.

By today's standards, it may have been crude, undisciplined and at times shockingly irreverent, but those are not the things one notices when one reads the book of Acts. What grips the imagination is not the lack of prestige but the demonstration of power. In that day, God moved in response to prayer. Miracles attended the saving power of Jesus Christ. Within the spreading fires of that church's influence, not only were the lost redeemed, but the lame walked, the blind received their sight and the oppressed were delivered from demonic powers. It was a fellowship of believers admittedly inperfect but vibrantly and dynamically alive. It may have been despised by the society around it, but no one ever accused it of being boring, dull or dead.

Those early Christians were more interested in manifesting the power of the Holy Spirit in their midst than in maintaining orderly worship services. They were more concerned with Christian love than correct liturgy, more concerned with being found faithful than being found popular. ". . . for with regard to this sect we know that everywhere it is spoken against" (Acts 28:22).

Comparing the New Testament church with ours today, it seems obvious that one of two things must have happened. Either God deliberately deprived the church of the power of Pentecost, with all its supernatural gifts and powers (a rationalization we hear over and over), or else the church has somehow lost contact with Pentecost as a vital, continuing experience.

The second proposition is the true one. The resurgence of Pentecostal power in our day proves it.

Even a hasty survey of church history clearly indicates that the charismatic gifts never completely died out of the church. Though consistently ignored, they have always been present, blazing up into public view during times of renewed religious fervor or revival. For example, back in the second century, a revival in the church, led by Montanus of Ardabau, captured the attention of many Christians who felt the spiritual fires within the church were burning at too low an ebb. During the peak of the Montanus revival, all the charismatic gifts appeared, including speaking in tongues. Two renowned church fathers, Tertullian and Iraneus, found much in the movement which was favorable, but the church official-dom in Rome considered the revival a threat to its authority and declared Montanism a heresy.

The *Encyclopedia Britannica* states that glossolalia

(speaking in tongues) "recurs in Christian revivals of every age, e.g., among the mendicant friars of the thirteenth century, among the Jansenists and early Quakers, the converts of Wesley and Whitefield, the persecuted Protestants of the Covennes and the Irvingites" (Volume 27, pp. 9-10, 11th edition).

The Irvingites were 19th century forerunners of the current recipients of the charismatic gifts. The Reverend Edward Irving was pastor of a Presbyterian church in London, England, in 1822, when his preaching on the need for a "new Pentecost" began to attract wide attention. By 1833, his emphasis upon the charismatic gifts had become too great (people had begun to speak in tongues!), and he was deposed from the Presbyterian ministry for heresy and moved to Scotland. But among his wide-spread following a new denomination was formed called the Catholic Apostolic Church and stress upon the charismatic gifts was continued.

The Irvingites proclaimed the necessity of the Pentecostal experience and stressed the certainty of Christ's second coming. From Scotland they established branch congregations in England, Germany and the United States. At its peak, the denomination is said to have numbered over 50,000 adherents. But when the last of the original leaders passed away in 1901, no attempt was made to replace them, and most of the members dispersed to other denominations.

The Pentecostal movement in the United States had its beginning in the year 1900 with the determination of a young Methodist minister named Charles F. Parham to recapture the power and vitality of the church of the New Testament. Opening a Bible school in an abandoned mansion in Topeka, Kansas, he and his students committed themselves to a thorough study of the

Scriptures to try and discover the secret to apostolic power. In December of that year, Parham gave his students an assignment to study every account of the Holy Spirit being received in the book of Acts, to discover if there was some overlooked factor common to them all.

The students, each doing his own study independently, all came to the same conclusion. Five times in the book of Acts, there is an account of the Holy Spirit being received. In three of these accounts—four if you include Paul's conversion—there was the appearance of the gift of tongues. (The students assumed that since Paul had the gift of tongues and testified to it in his first Corinthian letter, it probably came at the time he received the Holy Spirit [Acts 9:17].)

Backed by this strong scriptural evidence, Parham and his students prayed to receive the baptism in the Holy Spirit with the gift of tongues. The first person spoke in tongues on New Year's Eve, 1900. On January 3rd, Parham and a number of others also received the baptism and spoke in tongues.

From this modest beginning, the revival spread in 1906 to California, touching off the famed Azusa Street revival in Los Angeles. The Azusa revival lasted for three years with thousands of people from all over North America receiving the pentecostal experience of the Holy Spirit. A number of the present-day Pentecostal denominations trace their beginnings to that revival. (For more detailed accounts of Pentecostal beginnings read John Sherrill's *They Speak With Other Tongues*, Fleming H. Revell, Old Tappan, New Jersey.)

The Pentecostal movement grew at a phenomenal rate, spreading rapidly across the world. In just a little over fifty years, membership reached nearly 10 million. Strong on faith and short on patience, these small unlettered congregations came manifesting more of the dynamic power of the New Testament church than any Christian movement in centuries. Yet, despite their phenomenal growth, the Pentecostals were such a radical departure from the mainstream of Protestant tradition that the more established denominations viewed them with suspicion and even open hostility. So with their message ignored and their cries for a return to a charismatic ministry scoffed at, the Pentecostals drew their skirts of holiness about themselves and, shaking the dust of orthodoxy's doubt from their feet, became absorbed in a ministry to the multitudes whom the "respectable" churches passed by on the other side.

But today the charismatic revival has spilled over the boundaries so carefully drawn about it by its critics and is igniting fires in all major denominations, including the Roman Catholic. Bishop Lesslie Newbigin, a former president of the World Council of Churches, was one of the first outstanding churchmen to acknowledge the significance of this movement. He places it on an equal footing with traditional Protestantism and Roman Catholicism. In his book, *The Household of God*, he wrote:

> Catholicism and Orthodox Protestantism, however deeply they have differed from one another, have been at one in laying an immense stress on that in the Christian religion which is given and unalterable... Catholicism has laid its primary stress upon the given structure, Protestantism upon the given message.... It is necessary, however, to recognize that there is *a third stream* of Christian tradition which... has a distinct character of its own... its central element is the conviction that the

17

Christian life is a matter of the experienced power and presence of the Holy Spirit today ... that if we would answer the question, "Where is the Church?" we must ask, "Where is the Holy Spirit recognizably present with power?" ... for want of a better word I propose to refer to this type of Christian faith and life as the Pentecostal.[1]

Other leading churchmen have come to recognize the significance of this movement of the Spirit of God which was once dismissed as the enthusiasm of a cult. Dr. Henry Pitney Van Dusen, former president of Union Theological Seminary in New York, in a *Life* Magazine article of June 6, 1958, describes what he calls a "third, mighty arm of Christendom."

Its groups preach a direct Biblical message readily understood. They commonly promise an immediate life-transforming experience of the Living-God-In-Christ which is far more significant to many individuals than the version of it found in conventional churches. ... They shepherd their converts in an intimate, sustaining group-fellowship; a feature of every vital Christian renewal since the Holy Spirit descended on the disciples at the first Pentecost. They place strong emphasis upon the Holy Spirit—so neglected by many traditional Christians—as the immediate, potent presence of God in each human soul and in the Christian Fellowship.

Until lately, other Protestants regarded the movement as a temporary and passing phenome-

[1] Newbigin, *The Household of God* (S.C.M. Press, 1957), pp. 87-88.

non, not worth much mention. Now there is a growing, serious recognition of its true dimension and probable permanence. The tendency to dismiss its Christian message as inadequate is being replaced by a chastened readiness to investigate the secrets of its mighty sweep.[2]

In John Sherrill's book, *They Speak With Other Tongues*, Dr. Van Dusen makes an even more remarkable statement:

> I have come to feel...that the Pentecostal movement with its emphasis upon the Holy Spirit, is more than just another revival. It is a revolution in our day. It is a revolution comparable in importance with the establishment of the original Apostolic Church and with the Protestant Reformation.[3]

The late Reverend Samuel Shoemaker, shortly before his death, published a final article in The Episcopalian, a respected publication of the Protestant Episcopal Church in the U.S.A., entitled, "Can Our Kind of Church Change Our Kind of World?" In it Shoemaker said:

> Whatever the old-new phenomenon of "speaking in tongues" means, it is amazing that it should break out, not only in Pentecostal groups, but among Episcopalians, Lutherans, and Presbyterians. I have not had this experience myself. I have seen people who have, and it has blessed them and given

[2] Used by permission
[3] Sherrill, *They Speak With Other Tongues* (Old Tappan, New Jersey; Fleming H. Revell Company, 1965). p. 30.

them power they did not have before. I do not profess to understand this phenomenon. But I am fairly sure it indicates the Holy Spirit's presence in a life, as smoke from a chimney indicates a fire below. I know it means God is trying to get through into the church, staid and stuffy and self-centered as it often is, with the kind of power that will make it radiant and exciting and self-giving. We should seek to understand and be reverent toward this phenomenon, rather than to ignore or scorn it.

This rising tide of publicity and literature on the charismatic movement simply points to the ever-increasing influence it is having on Christianity. All over the world the church's spiritual pulse is being quickened by this new Pentecost.

CHAPTER 2

What is the baptism in the Holy Spirit?

The baptism in the Holy Spirit is a second encounter with God (the first is conversion) in which the Christian begins to receive the supernatural power of the Holy Spirit into his life. Jesus promised this power to his disciples when he said,

> You shall receive power when the Holy Spirit has come upon you; and you shall be my witnesses in Jerusalem and in all Judea and Samaria and to the end of the earth—Acts 1:8.

This promise was fulfilled at Pentecost when the Holy Spirit fell on the one hundred and twenty gathered in the upper room.

> They were all filled with the Holy Spirit and began to speak in other tongues, as the Spirit gave them utterance—Acts 2:4.

This second experience of the power of God, which we call the baptism in the Holy Spirit, is given for the purpose of equipping the Christian with God's power for service. It is the spiritual baptism from Jesus Himself, in which He begins to exercise His sovereign possession, control and use of us in supernatural fashion, through the Holy Spirit.

By way of illustration, let us point out that the New Testament describes both baptism in water and the baptism in the Holy Spirit. In Matthew 3:11, John the Baptist says,

> I baptize you with water for repentance, but he who is coming after me is mightier than I . . . he (Jesus) will baptize you with the Holy Spirit and with fire.

In Acts 1:4-5 Jesus says,

> For John baptized with water, but before many days you shall be baptized with the Holy Spirit.

And in his first sermon, preached on the day of Pentecost, Peter tells the multitude,

> Repent, and be baptized (water baptism) . . . for the forgiveness of your sins; and you shall receive the gift (baptism) of the Holy Spirit—Acts 2:38.

According to Scripture, these two baptisms are indicative of two separate, major experiences of the power of God. The first is conversion; the sinner's acceptance of Jesus Christ as Lord and Savior which brings salvation. He (the repentant sinner) gives testimony to his response to the gospel and his acceptance of Christ by receiving baptism in water for the remission of sins. Here, we see the new believer as the *object* of God's redemption. But the Lord is not satisfied with our conversion alone; He has promised us power to be His witnesses. So, a second time we are confronted with the power of God; this time in the baptism in the Holy Spirit through which the Christian is brought into a deeper relationship with Christ and the Holy Spirit for the purpose of making him—not an *object*—but an *instrument* of redemption.

The two baptisms may be compared as follows:

Christian Baptism by immersion in water
1. The candidate: the penitent believer (Matthew 28:19, Acts 2:38).
2. The baptismal element: water (Acts 8:36-38).
3. The baptizer: man—a preacher, evangelist, deacon (Acts 8:38).
4. The purpose: a witness to conversion and the remission of sins (Acts 2:38, Acts 22:16).
5. The result: salvation and entry into the body of Christ (Mark 16:16, Galatians 3:27).

Baptism in the Holy Spirit
1. The candidate: the baptized believer (Acts 2:38, Acts 8:14-17).
2. The baptismal element: the Holy Spirit (Mark 1:8).
3. The baptizer: Jesus Christ (Matthew 3:11, Mark 1:8).
4. The purpose: to endue the Christian with power (Acts 1:8, Luke 24:49).
5. The result: reception of the Holy Spirit with accompanying gifts and powers (Acts 2:4, Acts 8:14-17, 1 Corinthians 12:4-13).

CHAPTER 3

Why is the baptism in the Holy Spirit so important?

Jesus considered the baptism in the Holy Spirit so important that He expressly forbade His disciples to begin their ministry until they had received it. He knew it was essential for them to have the power which baptism in the Holy Spirit provides.

> And while staying with them he charged them not to depart from Jerusalem, but to wait for the promise of the Father, which, he said, "you heard from me, for John baptized with water, but before many days you shall be baptized with the Holy Spirit"—Acts 1:4-5.

There are many reasons why the baptism in the Holy Spirit is important. Rufus Moseley listed the following reasons in a little pamphlet entitled, "The Gift of The Holy Spirit."

(1) It is only through this Heavenly gift empowering us, guiding us, and transforming us that we have immediate union with the glorified Jesus and are given power to do His work and His will and to grow up into His likeness. As blessed as was the ministry of Jesus in the flesh, and as glorious as was His redemptive work in Gethsemane and Calvary, and His ministry during the

resurrection appearances, all this was preparatory to what was given to Jesus with power to impart when He ascended into the presence of the Father, and took His place upon the throne of the universe.

(2) If Jesus had remained on earth until now, with all His power to heal everyone He touched and everyone who touched Him, and had continued to perform all His mighty miracles, He still could have been only at one place at a time. People in their selfishness would have run over each other to get to Him. But since He went into glory and received the gift of the Father with power to share it with those who believe and obey, He has become omnipresent. Moreover, He has power not only to be with His disciples always, giving them what to say and what to do concerning everything they need to do unto the end of the world, but also power to come within and reproduce Himself in terms of all the capabilities of each one of us. Now He can give Himself totally to each one of us without neglecting any of the rest of us.

(3) Through ineffable union now, open to every believing and obedient disciple of Jesus, every one of us finds himself on the opposite kind of a cross from His. He was put upon a cross of shame; we, through happily yielding and responding to Him, are put upon a cross of highest honor. He was put upon a cross of agony; He puts us upon a cross of bliss. He was put upon a cross of death; He puts us upon a cross of life. When Jesus hung upon the cross of shame and agony and desertion, He gave up the Holy Breath or Holy Ghost; when we are put upon the cross by the Holy Spirit we receive the Holy Breath and are filled with the Holy Ghost.

(4) The Holy Spirit is the only Consciousness that knows Jesus and is capable of revealing Him as He is. All human philosophies and theologies tend to whittle Him

down to fit their own molds. The Holy Spirit changes us to fit the heavenly mold.

(5) The Holy Spirit, by revealing Jesus as He is, at the same time reveals us as we are. We are convicted of sin and incompleteness by seeing His sinlessness and perfection. As we see ourselves as we are, and see Him as He is, and make the acknowledgment, the miracle of forgiveness and cleansing and transformation occurs. He does not leave us in our nakedness; He furnishes the covering. He does not condemn us; He comes to our rescue. As we only know the mistakes in mathematics by knowing mathematics, it is only by knowing the truth that we can correct the mistakes. So the knowing of Jesus reveals the sin and the lack, and at the same time cleanses us and makes us whole.

(6) It is through the Holy Spirit that we are guided into all truth and shown things to come (John 16:13) and given power to overcome.

(7) Through the gift of the Holy Spirit, the body becomes consciously the Lord's. Here it is realized that the Lord is for the body, and the body is for the Lord. We become not only spirit of His spirit, mind of His mind, and soul of His soul, but we also become bone of His bone, flesh of His flesh, hands of His hands, feet of His feet, eyes of His eyes, ears of His ears, tongue of His tongue, and everything of His Perfect Everything. The body will never feel as it should as long as it feels itself. As the body is for the Lord and the Lord for the body, the body only feels as it ought to feel when it is feeling the Lord, and the Lord is never happy about the body except in having charge of it and imparting to it the health and the blessing of His presence.

Many other reasons for the importance of the baptism

in the Holy Spirit could be listed. Others will become apparent as you read further in the book.

CHAPTER 4

Is baptism in the Holy Spirit essential for salvation?

No, baptism in the Holy Spirit is *not* essential for salvation. Salvation, or conversion, or the acceptance of Christ as Lord and Savior, is a separate, prior experience. Millions of Christians who love and serve Jesus Christ as Savior have not received the baptism in the Holy Spirit. The New Testament makes it plain that baptism in the Holy Spirit is a second work of grace which follows conversion.

> Philip went down to a city of Samaria, and proclaimed to them the Christ.... But when they believed Philip as he preached good news about the kingdom of God and the name of Jesus Christ, they were baptized, both men and women.
>
> Now when the apostles at Jerusalem heard that Samaria had received the word of God, they sent to them Peter and John, who came down and prayed for them that they might receive the Holy Spirit; for it had not yet fallen on any of them, but they had only been baptized in the name of the Lord Jesus—Acts 8:5, 12, 14-16.

At times, baptism in the Holy Spirit may come immediately following conversion, like in Acts 10, when

Peter preached to the household of Cornelius. On that occasion, as Peter preached faith in Christ and forgiveness of sins through His name (Acts 10:43), those who heard, believed, and were immediately filled with the Holy Spirit (Acts 10:44-48).

Peter's statement in Acts 2:38 seems to indicate that baptism in the Holy Spirit should immediately follow water baptism. While this may be ideally true and occasionally happens today (a missionary friend related how young converts in Mexico came up out of the baptismal waters praising God in tongues and prophesying), it is not common. Most Christians today receive the baptism in the Holy Spirit only after instructions and specific prayer.

Again, let us state that while we know the baptism in the Holy Spirit to be an important Christian doctrine and a vastly needed Christian experience for bringing New Testament power back into the church, it is *not* essential for salvation.

CHAPTER 5

I had a wonderful conversion experience and assumed I received the Holy Spirit then. Doesn't conversion bring the Holy Spirit?

Certainly the Holy Spirit is present in conversion. Paul says, "No one can say 'Jesus is Lord' except by the Holy Spirit" (1 Corinthians 12:3). We know that every Christian experiences a measure of the Holy Spirit's power. But the Scriptures plainly teach there is spiritual power available beyond our experience of conversion. Obviously, Paul was converted on the road to Damascus, but the Lord sent Ananias to him to pray for him to get his sight back and to *be filled with the Holy Spirit* (Acts 9:17). And while the Samaritan Christians were soundly converted under Philip's teaching, still it was through prayer and the laying on of hands that they received the Holy Spirit (Acts 8:14-17).

Let us stress that this deeper experience of the Holy Spirit in no way refutes or denies any experience the Christian may have had before. It simply opens unto us a whole new realm of spiritual possibilities.

Many Christians seem to feel that since their conversion was so wonderful, this must be all that God has for them. Yet, many of those same Christians confess to a lack of boldness and a lack of power.

The baptism in the Holy Spirit is not a saving

experience for the non-Christian; it is an empowering experience for the Christian in order that he may be supernaturally equipped to perform his ministry.

Reverend Dennis Bennett observes that in these days of the devil's wrath it is almost tragic to bring a person to Jesus Christ and stop short of praying him through to the baptism in the Holy Spirit. "It's like recruiting a man into the army," Bennett declares, "and not giving him any weapons to fight with. He goes into battle unarmed and may soon end up a prisoner of the enemy."

Bennett also has a unique way of picturing the difference between the Christian's *having* the Holy Spirit in conversion and *receiving* Him in terms of the baptism in the Holy Spirit.

"A man may push his way past my secretary and come into my office and sit down while I am very busy at my desk. I know he is there, but continue working, not acknowledging his presence. After a few minutes my telephone rings and someone on the other end of the line asks, 'Have you a man in your office?' and proceeds to describe my visitor. I reply, 'Yes, he's here, but I haven't laid aside my work to welcome him. I haven't *received* him yet.'"

"But then suppose," Bennett continues, "I lay aside my work and give my visitor a cordial welcome and devote to him my undivided attention and ask him, 'Why are you here and how may I serve you?' Then my visitor may rise to his feet with a glad smile and shake my hand and say, 'Oh, I'm so glad you finally *received* me, for I have a check for you for one million dollars and I want to give it to you. And I have an important message from a friend whom you haven't seen in a long time, plus so many other good things I want to share with you, *now that you have received me*.'"

So it is with many Christians. They have the Holy Spirit present in their lives, but He sits quietly waiting to be *received*. They have not yet made Him fully welcome, nor given Him their full attention, nor tried to discover the purpose of His coming, thus robbing themselves of the gifts and powers He wishes to bestow. They are like the Ephesian disciples whom Paul asked, "Did you *receive* the Holy Spirit when you believed?" (Acts 19:2). The baptism in the Holy Spirit is *receiving* Him with power into our lives.

CHAPTER 6

Is every Christian meant to have the baptism in the Holy Spirit?

The New Testament apostles thought so. "Did you receive the Holy Spirit when you believed?" (Acts 19:2) seemed to be a kind of watchword with the early church. And Peter's plea in Acts 2:38 for both the acceptance of Christ as Lord and the receiving of the Holy Spirit is followed by a universal promise: "For the promise is to you and to your children and to all that are far off, everyone whom the Lord our God calls to him" (Acts 2:39).

When Philip's preaching in Samaria, as recorded in Acts 8, resulted in the conversion of multitudes to Christ, the apostles in Jerusalem quickly sent down Peter and John to minister to the new converts that they might be filled with the Holy Spirit, "for it had not yet fallen on any of them, but they had only been baptized in the name of the Lord Jesus" (Acts 8:16).

It is important to note that while the apostles did not doubt the validity of the conversion of the Samaritans, still they were not content to leave them without this further vital experience of the power of God. Today, the majority of Christians seem to fit the description of those Samaritans. They have salvation but not the power to minister and witness which comes with Jesus' baptism in the Holy Spirit.

If you are a Christian, you can and should have the baptism in the Holy Spirit.

CHAPTER 7

My minister claims the age of miracles is past and that the charismatic gifts, including speaking in tongues and miracles of healing, are not meant for today. How can I answer him?

Well, you can love your minister for his sincerity, but his theology at this point is in error. Most ministers who were trained in liberal Bible colleges and seminaries had this same theory drilled into them. When I say this I include myself, for I was trained in such a seminary. We need to know how such theories came into being and to see that they are not based on Scripture. Hebrews 13:8 plainly states, "Jesus Christ is the same yesterday and today and for ever." As Rufus Moseley used to say, "This means that what Jesus was, He is; what He said, He says; and what He did, He does." Jesus still saves today, still heals today, still baptizes in the Holy Spirit today, and still performs miracles in answer to the prayer of faith today.

The belief that the age of miracles is past is commonly called dispensationalism. Dispensationalism claims that God has tried various expedients with man, each one having been completely abandoned before the next one was attempted so that divine workings in one age or dispensation do not apply to the next. This faulty teaching has played literal havoc with the faith of millions of Christians, deluding them into believing that the supernatural power of God which wrought miracles in New Testament days is not available today.

Dispensationalism gained popular support, not because the Scriptures back it up, but because it seemed to offer a ready excuse for why the church today is not a miracle-working church. You can see it is far easier to claim that the age of miracles is past than to admit that the miraculous power of God is still available, but that the church lacks the devotion and faith necessary to bring them into manifestation.

Some dispensationalists claim the miracle gifts and powers were withdrawn at the close of the apostolic age (around 100 A.D.) when the last apostle and the last one upon whom an apostle laid his hands had died. The miracle gifts were but a temporary blessing bestowed by God to help get the struggling young church on its feet. Once the church was well established, God snatched the power away.

Others claim it was the completion of the New Testament (around 350 A.D.) which signalled the end of miracles. Once the New Testament was complete, God's revelation was finished, so the Holy Spirit gave up performing miracles and today confines His activity to the written word; a theory which has led some rather zealous devotees of this position to hold their New Testaments aloft and boast, "I can buy all the Holy Spirit there is for fifty cents."

Still others claim the miracles were needed only so long as the early Christians were superstitious and immature and needed "divine signs" to help them believe, but that the mature and enlightened church of today has no need of such signs and wonders. This last argument is so obviously contradicted by the anemic state of current Christianity that no thoughtful person can take it seriously. If there was ever a time when the church and the world stood in greater peril and need, if there was ever a time when the onslaughts of Satan were as great or when evil was running as rampant, history has failed to record it. We need every spiritual gift and power contained in God's arsenal in order to wage successful spiritual warfare today.

In seeking support for their arguments, dispensationalists often make reference to two passages of Scripture. One is 1 Corinthians 13:8-10; "As for prophecies, they will pass away; as for tongues, they will cease . . . when the perfect comes, the imperfect will pass away." The coming of "the perfect" is assumed to be the completion of the New Testament. After that, goodbye spiritual gifts!

True, Paul says the imperfect will pass away. But when? Paul knew nothing of a coming end of the apostolic age nor of a completed New Testament. In fact, there is nothing in his writings to indicate that he ever assumed there would be a written New Testament. The context makes it clear that the coming of the perfect was to be the return of Christ and the establishment of the Kingdom of God on earth when he (and we) would see Christ "face to face" and would "understand even as we are understood" (1 Corinthians 13:12).

The other scripture is 2 Timothy 4:20, "Trophimus I left ill at Miletus" which is offered as scriptural proof that miracles had ceased at that time since Paul was unable to heal Trophimus. But the fact that everyone prayed for does not receive healing is no more an indication that the miraculous power of God has been withdrawn than the fact that everyone hearing the message of salvation does not accept Christ is an indication that God has withdrawn His power to save. Just as there are many reasons why people do not respond to the gospel message, so there are many reasons why people do not respond miraculously when a prayer for healing is offered. The truth is, multitudes have been saved through preaching and multitudes have been healed of disease, filled with the Holy Spirit and are today experiencing the supernatural manifestations of the Holy Spirit, even as Jesus promised.

> These signs shall follow them that believe; in my name shall they cast out demons, they shall speak with new tongues... they shall lay hands on the sick, and they shall recover—Mark 16:17 *KJV*.

The dispensationalist, having eliminated a miracle-working God from his Christianity, is placed in a painful position when confronted with a miracle of healing. No matter that the one receiving healing glorifies God; no matter that friends and relatives may be brought to Christ through the miracle; no matter that the healing is fully consistent with the teachings of Jesus in the New Testament. The dispensationalist often resorts to the radical explanation of the miracle: "The devil did it." And in declaring a miracle of God to be a work of Satan, he performs an act of great spiritual danger, for his denunciation borders on blasphemy against the Holy Spirit, the one unforgivable sin.

In Matthew, chapter 12, when Jesus heals a blind and dumb demoniac, the Pharisees say, "It is only by Beelzebub, the prince of demons, that this man casts out demons" (verse 24), thus attributing a miracle wrought by the Holy Spirit to Satan. Listen to our Lord's solemn reply:

> Therefore I tell you, every sin and blasphemy will be forgiven men, but the blasphemy against the

Spirit will not be forgiven. And whoever says a word against the Son of man will be forgiven; but whoever speaks against the Holy Spirit will not be forgiven either in this age or in the age to come—Matthew 12:31-32.

One final comment on dispensationalism: Rufus Moseley once wisely observed, "If those who insist the age of miracles has ended had lived in Jesus' day, the age of miracles might never have begun." In other words, the skeptic who rejects the miracles today would have rejected them in Jesus' day. Miracles are no more believable simply because they happened hundreds of years ago. Unbelief is still the greatest hindrance to the manifestation of God's power. It thwarted even the ministry of Jesus when, in his own home town, they refused to believe and "took offense at him."

And he could do no mighty work there. . . . and he marveled because of their unbelief—Mark 6:5-6.

CHAPTER 8

How do you answer people who claim this experience is not normative to Christianity and that Jesus never spoke in tongues?

Neither argument carries much weight. First of all, how much importance should we place on whether or not a religious practice is currently "normative"? Christianity is not the normative religion of the world today, but this does not keep Christians from proclaiming Jesus Christ as the light of the world and believing that it is God's will for all men to come to a saving knowledge of Him. While the baptism in the Holy Spirit may not yet be normative in the church of our day, nevertheless it is growing by leaps and bounds. It was much more normative in the early church than is generally understood. A study of Scripture shows that Christians in Caesarea, Samaria, Ephesus, Rome, Corinth and Jerusalem received the Holy Spirit with speaking in tongues since either direct or indirect references point to the fact.

We know that the 120 in the upper room at Pentecost spoke in tongues as did the apostle Paul. From this group almost the entire leadership of the early church came. Obviously, as they ministered in the power of the Holy Spirit, the experience of tongues was a part of what they shared and passed on through prayer and the laying on of hands. Everywhere the Holy Spirit was received, the supernatural gifts, including tongues, followed.

While it is only in Paul's first Corinthian letter, chapters 12-14, that we find any lengthy discussion or teaching about tongues and the other charismatic gifts, this was not because the Corinthian Christians were the only Christians *experiencing* the gifts, but because they were the only ones *abusing* them.

By comparison, we assume the Lord's Supper was in widespread use throughout the New Testament church, but it is only in the same epistle, chapters ten and eleven, that any substantial teaching or instructions are given concerning communion. Here again, it was not use but abuse which led to the instructions. Yet, many Christians who have allowed Paul's criticism of the improper use of tongues to deny their validity and use in the church today would not dream of allowing Paul's criticism of the improper administration of the Lord's Supper to deny their right to the current observance of the Lord's Supper in their church.

As for the second part of the question, it is true that so far as we know Jesus never spoke in tongues. His relationship to the Father was unique and His praise to God perfect. Also, we should remember that speaking in tongues and its companion gift of interpretation are the two unique gifts identified with the age of the Holy Spirit which was ushered in at Pentecost. (All the other gifts had been manifested before.) What is significant for us to remember is that the baptism in the Holy Spirit, which Jesus Himself bestows, includes speaking in tongues. It was Jesus Himself who listed tongues as one of the "signs" which would accompany His followers: "And these signs will accompany those who believe: in my name they will cast out demons; *they will speak in new tongues ...*" (Mark 16:17). It was the Risen, Glorified Jesus who fulfilled His own prophecy by sending the Holy Spirit with speaking in tongues at Pentecost.

The baptism in the Holy Spirit with speaking in tongues was normative in the early church. We pray it will become normative in the church today.

CHAPTER 9

If the charismatic movement is really a revival sent from God, why is there opposition to it?

God deliver us from the day when the church has no critics and is at peace with the world! The times when the church has been most faithful and powerful have always been times of division, disturbance and criticism. Every great revival has had its critics, and this one is no exception. The outpouring of the Holy Spirit brings great problems because it brings great power. The devil is never content to let God's power go unchallenged.

It is not easy for church members, who for years have been complacent and satisfied in their religious habits, to admit something vital may have been missing from their religion. Norman Vincent Peale once observed in a sermon that the watchword of upper-middle-class Protestantism was "Don't do anything to rock the boat." Well, an outpouring of the Holy Spirit with gifts and powers does just exactly that. It rocks the boat. The witness of a Spirit-filled Christian often brings indictment against church members whose lives are relatively devoid of any spiritual power.

Also, part of the opposition to revival comes from ignorance. Many modern Christians are simply ignorant of scriptural teaching on the Holy Spirit. On becoming familiar with New Testament teaching, many of these same people come to see that what is happening today in this revival is scriptural, and they lose their objections to it.

When confronted by the power of God, we have two choices. One is to claim the revival is false and reject it. The other is to take a receptive stand, respond with joy to what God is doing in our day, and let the revival sweep over us.

CHAPTER 10

I've seen people who have the baptism in the Holy Spirit and who speak in tongues do and say many unloving things. Doesn't this lack of love show that the fruit of the Spirit is more important than the gifts?

The baptism in the Holy Spirit opens the way to many wonderful gifts of God, but it does not provide instant holiness or perfection. Far from it. We must not confuse the gifts of the Spirit with the fruit of the Spirit. The fruit of the Spirit which Paul lists in Galatians 5:22-33 is an evidence, not of the baptism in the Holy Spirit, but of conversion or the new birth (see 1 John 3:14). And it is not always quick to appear in the life of a Christian, even one baptized in the Holy Spirit. Just as one may manifest a measure of the fruit of the Spirit, yet experience none of the charismatic gifts, it is also possible (although not desirable) for one baptized in the Holy Spirit to manifest gifts of the Spirit, yet little fruit. But its very nature fruit takes time to produce. Paul criticized the church at Corinth because he saw little evidence of the *fruit* of the Spirit, yet he said, "I give thanks to God always for you... that you are not lacking in any spiritual gift" (1 Corinthians 1:4-7).

On the other hand, no matter if the fruit of the Spirit is in evidence in the life of the Christian (and ideally this should always be the case), without the baptism in the

Holy Spirit with its attendant gifts that person is missing out on a great measure of Divine power which will equip him for a more powerful Christian witness.

Of course, the ideal is for the Christian to be fully manifesting both the gifts and the fruit of the Spirit. To advocate either without the other is to err. The two go hand in hand. This is why we find Paul's beautiful Psalm to love in 1 Corinthians 13—and remember love is a fruit and not a gift of the Spirit—sandwiched neatly in between chapters 12 and 14 in 1 Corinthians. Many Christians, though able to quote the 13th chapter by memory, remain woefully ignorant of chapters 12 and 14. Paul offers the best of both possible worlds in chapter 14, verse 1, when he says, "Make love your aim (or do not be content until you manifest the fruit of the Spirit), and earnestly desire the spiritual gifts" (or do not seek the fruit alone, but the gifts of the Spirit as well). Many Christians seem to read that verse as if it said, "Make love your aim, and earnestly reject spiritual gifts." When speaking of the fruit and gifts of the Spirit, what Paul advocates is not "either-or" but "both-and."

The major point to remember in order not to confuse the gifts and fruit of the Spirit is: the *gifts* are supernaturally bestowed by the Spirit, being miraculously manifested in the believer at a specific time and for a specific purpose. The *fruit* of the Spirit can more accurately be described as traits developing in Christian character; qualities in the Christian's life which—although made possible only by God's grace—develop and mature slowly.

People who have not yet come to understand the experience of the baptism in the Holy Spirit often cite the faults and weaknesses of Spirit-filled Christians (the lack of the fruit of the Spirit, if you will) as a valid reason for

46

not seeking the baptism. Their criticisms should help to keep us humble. But they should not let such criticisms turn them aside from seeking the supernatural power of God. To do so is as foolish as accepting a non-Christian's criticism of an imperfect Christian as valid proof that there is nothing to Christianity.

Paul's criticism of the abuse of tongues in 1 Corinthians 14 is often used by the skeptic to rule out the exercise of the gifts entirely. But while Paul did criticize the undisciplined display of tongues there, we should remember he was speaking to people who had received the ability to pray in tongues, advising them how to use the manifestation wisely, for the upbuilding of the church. He was neither disparaging the proper manifestation of tongues nor suggesting that it be removed from the worship service.

> "So, my brethren, earnestly desire to prophesy, and do not forbid speaking in tongues; but all things should be done decently and in order"—1 Corinthians 14:39-40.

CHAPTER 11

Why do Spirit-filled Christians become so talkative about their faith and so aggressive in their witness? Don't they know this embarrasses other Christians?

There is some truth in this observation. At times Spirit-filled Christians are "pushy," and this may seem unfortunate. But the major cause of this complaint may not be the Spirit-filled, witnessing Christian so much as the lack of conviction or Christian testimony on the part of the lukewarm church member. As Rufus Moseley once dryly observed, "The average spiritual temperature in the church is so low that when a healthy man comes along everyone thinks he has a fever."

Often the change within the life of a person who has received the baptism in the Holy Spirit is so remarkable he finds it difficult not to talk about it. He has something to witness to and it may be hard to keep him quiet. No doubt there are times when enthusiasm may get ahead of wisdom and deep convictions may strain the limits of conventional church behavior. Yet, if such testimony proves embarrassing, the real problem may not lie so much with the one witnessing as with those listening. Why shouldn't Christians share with the world and with one another the glory and power of God? What an indictment on the Church of Jesus Christ that many Christians find themselves embarrassed at personal testimony!

A minister friend, Reverend J. P. Murray of West Lorne, Ontario, tells of returning to a former pastorate to visit a family where a grown son was obviously head-over-heels in love. One evening as they sat talking, Murray turned to the boy. "John," he asked, "how long have you been in love with Mary?" John blushed furiously. "How did you know I was in love?" he stammered. Murray answered with a smile, "I know because no matter what we may be talking about, somehow you manage to bring Mary's name into the conversation."

Those who have a dynamic and vital relationship to Jesus Christ through the Holy Spirit are like that. They have a way of including His name in their conversation. It may well prove an embarrassment to lukewarm Christians. It also indicates those who testify may have something wonderful to share.

> So they called them and charged them not to speak or teach at all in the name of Jesus. But Peter and John answered them, "Whether it is right in the sight of God to listen to you rather than to God, you must judge; *for we cannot but speak of what we have seen and heard*"—Acts 4:18-20.

CHAPTER 12

Many claim that this charismatic movement is just fanaticism. How can you be sure it is from God?

The same claim has been lodged against every revival in the history of Christianity; so there is no reason to expect this current revival will not have its share of critics. It has. Traditionally, the institutional church has been the bulwark of conservatism. Anything new or different is automatically suspect. (Someone has described a conservative as a man who believes that nothing should ever be done for the first time.)

It is not difficult to understand the logic behind the accusation of fanaticism, or that the whole revival is spurious. Institutional leaders have always found it safer to look backward than forward. Prophets and spiritual leaders caught up in fresh moves of the Spirit of God have always suffered persecution until their religious movements eventually gained the respect of society. Then they became heroes and "fathers of the faith." Until then they were troublemakers and fanatics.

Someone has described a fanatic as "one who has stronger convictions than I have." The definition has a large element of truth in it. Frankly, we live in an age of "watered-down" Christianity. A man willing to give his life for his country is a patriot. Let the same man confess a willingness to die for Jesus Christ, and he's a fanatic. The current brand of Christianity hawked by most churches makes few demands on people. It may make an effort to comfort the afflicted, but no effort to afflict the comfortable. The easiest thing in the world to join is the church. It is more difficult to gain membership in most lodges and service organizations than it is to join a church.

With this kind of spirit and background existing in a large part of Christendom, any claim to fresh and vital Christian experience which drastically alters the lives of those involved is bound to be labelled in many corners as "fanaticism." Lukewarm church members are the modern counterpart of those whom Jesus described in Matthew 13, quoting Isaiah:

> You shall indeed hear but never understand, and you shall indeed see but never perceive. For this people's heart has grown dull, and their ears are heavy of hearing, and their eyes they have closed, lest they should perceive with their eyes, and hear with their ears, and understand with their heart, and turn for me to heal them—Matthew 13:13-15.

How can you be sure the charismatic movement is from God? Well, if you are willing to apply them, there are several simple tests to help determine the truth. Here are three of them:

(1) Is the movement scriptural? Does it coincide with the teachings of the New Testament and the life and practice of the New Testament church? Any movement which claims to be of God and yet cannot be supported by Scriptures should be suspect.

(2) The Scripture says, "By their fruits you will know

them," so look at the lives of those involved. Are they better people morally and spiritually than they were before? Are they stronger Christians? Is God more real to them? Are they better witnesses to Jesus Christ?

(3) Does the charismatic movement glorify Jesus Christ? If it is really of God and empowered by the Holy Spirit, it will exalt Jesus Christ. Is Jesus Christ occupying a more central position in the lives of those involved in the movement? If so, it is of God.

If the answer to these three questions is yes, then the charismatic movement is of God.

CHAPTER 13

Isn't the baptism in the Holy Spirit meant primarily for the unsophisticated believer? Doesn't one have to be of a particular emotional temperament to be receptive to this kind of experience?

No. Peter makes this plain when he told the people on the day of Pentecost:

> Repent, and be baptized every one of you in the name of Jesus Christ for the forgiveness of your sins; and you shall receive the gift of the Holy Spirit. For the promise is to you and to your children *and to all that are far off, every one* whom the Lord our God calls to him—Acts 2:38-39.

Just as every person can know Jesus Christ as Lord and Savior, so we believe every Christian can receive the baptism in the Holy Spirit. It is not an experience for a particular type but for all types. The only prerequisite is that you must be a Christian.

Among the millions of people who have received the baptism in the Holy Spirit in the last few decades, we find representatives of every conceivable profession and walk of life and every emotional temperament and personality type. God is no respecter of persons nor of social or economic strata. In the ranks of Spirit-filled believers, we find doctors, lawyers, psychiatrists, college professors, scientists, clergymen, military personnel (including admirals and generals), business executives and politicians, laborers, housewives, college students, and children.

Emotional temperament, personality or religious background may play a part in how quickly a Christian yields himself to the Holy Spirit and may have some effect on the physical response to the Spirit's working, but they have no bearing on the spiritual reality or power implicit in the baptism in the Holy Spirit.

The Holy Spirit does not change human personality, but His abiding Presence certainly enhances it. The Spirit makes dull people bright and bright people brilliant. And when we see one whose personality was bound and crippled by selfishness and fear set free by the Holy Spirit's power, they may appear to have actually undergone a personality transformation.

But the Holy Spirit is a gentleman. He works in our lives only to the extent that we are willing. He prompts and leads and woos and persuades, but He does not force. To become a Christian a person must will or want to accept Christ, and he can. To be filled with the Holy Spirit a Christian must will or want to receive, and he can. Baptism in the Holy Spirit is available for every Christian, regardless of personality traits or temperament.

CHAPTER 14

If the miraculous gifts are meant for today, why can't we empty all the hospitals and sick beds and provide miraculous answers for all the needs of mankind?

This is a question commonly bandied about among Christians who feel the age of miracles is past. Its weakness lies in the implication that the miracle-working power of God is like magic, and that the signs and wonders of God's power can be divorced from the gospel message. Let us recast the same question in terms of salvation: If Jesus is the Son of God with power to save, why isn't the whole world Christian? The immediate answer is that salvation is dependent upon man's response to the gospel message.

Potentially, what both questions ask is possible, for *potentially*, every human need has been met in the grace of God revealed through the atonement of Jesus Christ. Christ died for *all* men. The intent of God to establish a society on earth where every need is met through His love and grace is clearly revealed in New Testament teaching. It is called the Kingdom of God. Jesus demonstrated it in His ministry, proclaimed its proximity, and we pray for its manifestation every time we pray the Lord's prayer: "Thy kingdom come... on earth."

But we must also recognize that *the promises of God are conditional.* They require the surrender of man's will to the will of God. Man's full response in faith to the promises of God involves submission and obedience. In fact, it necessitates a kind of death; a crucifixion of the old nature that the divine life and nature of Jesus Christ may be formed in us.

We find no basis in Scripture for assuming that the blessings and miracles of God are automatic, or that they will be bestowed upon those who are unbelieving, indifferent, or unrepentant and who have neither sought God's will nor surrendered their lives to Him. God's blessings are contingent upon man's repentance and surrender and his turning to God in prayer and faith. As the Lord reminded Solomon,

> If my people who are called by my name humble themselves, and pray and seek my face, and turn from their wicked ways, then I will hear from heaven, and will forgive their sin and heal their land—2 Chronicles 7:14.

The time may soon be upon us when mass healing miracles will result in the emptying of entire hospitals. This has already been seen in vision and promised by the Lord in prophecy. It is an established fact that even today, where great revivals are in progress—such as the one in Indonesia—mass healing miracles have already taken place.

Miracles of healing and other supernatural evidences of the power of God are the "signs" which, from the age of the Apostles, were meant to follow "those who believe" (Mark 16:17). Today, we find them occurring with ever-increasing frequency and believe they foreshadow the sinless and miraculous kingdom which Jesus Christ will set up on earth when He returns.

CHAPTER 15

Can one receive the baptism in the Holy Spirit and not be aware that he has received it?

Generally speaking, the answer to this question is no, one cannot receive the baptism in the Holy Spirit and not know he has received it. But to be more precise, we must qualify that answer in three ways:

(1) On rare occasions people *have* received the baptism in the Holy Spirit with speaking in tongues and, although they knew something strange and wonderful had taken place, did not know what had happened to them. They had never heard of the baptism in the Holy Spirit and so had no way to define the experience. In such cases, the baptism usually comes in some deep moment of prayer or during a time of spontaneous praise to God.

We know one friend who went forward in a meeting for what she thought was to be prayer for healing. She had misunderstood the minister's invitation, which had been for those seeking the baptism in the Holy Spirit. As she sat in the appointed place, people gathered around and began praying for her. Suddenly, she felt her tongue begin to thrash around in her mouth and found herself speaking in tongues in the midst of a glorious feeling of love and power. But it was only after friends had explained her experience that she understood what had happened. But again, let us stress that such experiences are rare.

(2) A second part of the answer is directed to yet another group of people. There are those Christians who seem to feel that the baptism in the Holy Spirit is a blessing which God mysteriously and secretly bestows here and there and who wonder if, at some time in their Christian walk or experience, they received this blessing without being aware of it. They wonder if they received the baptism when they accepted Christ or at some point when they made a special commitment to God. I believe it is fairly safe to say to all such persons, "If you doubt that you've received the baptism in the Holy Spirit, you haven't." This encounter with God's Holy Spirit is too charged with Divine life and power for us to take it for granted or to assume it came to us unnoticed. And this is one of the reasons we look for the manifestation of speaking in tongues. It is concrete evidence that the person speaking has been baptized in the Holy Spirit.

(3) A third part of the answer to this question deals with those who have actively sought the baptism in the Holy Spirit, have received prayer for the baptism and have even spoken a strange word or two in tongues, but doubt that they have really received the baptism. Many, many people experience this problem. They have received the baptism but are not yet sure of their experience. They haven't spoken as fluently as their friends do, or their experience has not measured up to their expectations. If this is your situation, then let me assure you, yes, you have received the baptism in the Holy Spirit, but the devil is trying to talk you out of it. If you've spoken so much as one syllable in tongues, claim your experience by faith and persevere in prayer until you become fluent in your new language of praise.

So to summarize: On rare occasions, God does baptize people in the Holy Spirit, and they do not know what happened except that it was wonderful. Secondly, if a person has never sought the baptism, never spoken in tongues, yet wonders if maybe God baptized him without him being aware of it, no, he has *not* received. But thirdly, when a person actively seeks the baptism and is prayed for to receive, he may receive and even speak a few words in an unknown tongue, yet doubts, then *yes*, he has received, but the devil is doing his dead-level best to talk him out of it.

CHAPTER 16

Why is it that people baptized in the Holy Spirit are not in agreement on all points of doctrine?

The baptism in the Holy Spirit always results in significant changes in the theology of those who receive it, for the overwhelming reality of the Holy Spirit tends to make many previously held beliefs and doctrines insignificant. But we should remember that the baptism in the Holy Spirit is an enduement with power and an equipping for Christian service, not a ticket to omniscience. At many points, Spirit-filled Christians differ. But they are one hundred percent in agreement on the importance and significance of the baptism in the Holy Spirit.

Even the apostles did not always agree (see Acts 15, also Galatians 2:1-15). As great and wise as Paul was, he still admitted, "For now we see in a mirror dimly.... Now I know in part...(1 Corinthians 13:12). Yet, in spite of differences, there is a very precious fellowship and unity created among people baptized in the Holy Spirit. It is a unity born of the Holy Spirit and sustained by the Holy Spirit. Many of us believe it is in the charismatic movement that the greatest hope for true Christian unity lies.

One of the delights of receiving the baptism in the Holy Spirit is the freedom it brings concerning denominationalism. The bond of fellowship created by baptism in the

Holy Spirit tends to overshadow denominational differences and unite Christians at a level beyond their reach. I personally know Baptists, Methodists, Episcopalians, Lutherans, Congregationalists, Disciples of Christ, Presbyterians, Nazarenes, Pentecostal members of several varieties, as well as members of the United Church of Canada, Brethren, Moravian, Amish and Roman Catholics, all of whom are Spirit-filled. And when we meet and have fellowship, the dominant concern is not which denomination is right, but rather "How can we tell more people of the love of Jesus and the power of His Holy Spirit?"

CHAPTER 17

What is the baptism in the Holy Spirit meant to accomplish in us?

Essentially, the baptism in the Holy Spirit is a doorway leading from a natural realm into a supernatural realm of life and experience. The average Christian, although truly professing Christ, operates largely on his own power, making his own decisions, living by his own strength, and controlling his own life. But through the baptism in the Holy Spirit, the Christian steps out of this natural realm into a realm where he can begin to experience the *supernatural* gifts and powers of God's Holy Spirit.

The initial evidence of entering this supernatural realm is the ability to speak in other tongues. (See Section 2 for a discussion of tongues.) But that is just the beginning. If all that happened to the 120 at Pentecost had been that they began to speak in tongues, their experience would soon have been forgotten. The same is true today. If all that happens to one receiving the baptism in the Holy Spirit is that he speaks in tongues, then he is not forging ahead in faith in this powerful new realm into which God has ushered him. There are many other benefits and blessings awaiting him. The list that follows draws on the testimonies of many Spirit-filled Christians. While it is a typical list, it is by no means exhaustive.

1. *Baptism in the Holy Spirit often brings a stronger assurance of Salvation.*

Jesus said, "Unless one is born anew, he cannot see the kingdom of God" (John 3:3). Many Christians, when they accept Jesus Christ as Savior, do experience a deep conversion and the assurance that they belong to Christ. But for countless others, the assurance of their born-again experience does not occur until they are baptized in the Holy Spirit. As Paul says, "When we cry 'Abba, Father!' it is the Spirit himself bearing witness with our spirit that we are the children of God" (Romans 8:15-16).

Today, many members of the mainline Christian denominations, on hearing of the possibility of a more powerful, personal relationship with Jesus, have sought and found it through the baptism in the Holy Spirit.

The following testimony of one who recently received the baptism in the Holy Spirit is typical of many:

> For years I had been a faithful church member. I came to worship, I listened to sermons, I worked on committees, I served in every way I knew how, yet I was not satisfied. When I heard about the baptism in the Holy Spirit, I knew this was something I really needed. And when I received it, Jesus became much more real to me. Everything changed! I began to love people. The church services suddenly came to life. All the hymns and prayers became almost unbearably sweet. The sermons sounded as if we had a new minister, only he had been saying the same things all along. I was the one who was changed.

Yet, trying to explain this experience to those who have not experienced it themselves can be as difficult as trying to describe hot weather to Eskimos. In churches where worship and service are based on an intellectual assent to the gospel, where fellowship is determined by social and economic ties rather than on the common experience of personal redemption, the testimony of a Spirit-filled Christian—whose heart has been melted in the flame of a profoundly moving encounter with the Risen Lord as Baptizer and King—may be completely misunderstood or rejected. The lukewarm church member cannot really understand it until it happens to him.

2. *Baptism in the Holy Spirit brings a further crucifixion of "the old man."*

The baptism in the Holy Spirit brings with it a new spiritual sensitivity—a sensitivity which works more ways than one. Just as we become more aware of God's Presence within us, so do we also become more aware of the presence of sin. This increased sensitivity to sin is matched by a desire for personal holiness, but while the spirit is willing the flesh is often weak.

Potentially, we die to the old nature when we become Christians ("We know that our old self was crucified with him so that the sinful body might be destroyed and we might no longer be enslaved to sin"—Romans 6:6), but the realization of this crucifixion of the old man in our actual experience is another matter. While one may experience immediate deliverance from a particular illness, addiction or personal weakness as a result of being baptized in the Holy Spirit, and while new and unmistakable joy and power enter into one's life, still the battle against the "old man" continues to be waged in other areas of our lives. *There is no such thing as instant holiness.*

A friend, Enid Newman, once shared an experience which illustrates this point. One day while she was earnestly praying for God to make her more tolerant and loving, the Holy Spirit prompted her to claim a particular passage of Scripture as a personal promise, Ezekiel 36:26: "A new heart I will give you . . . I will take out of your flesh the heart of stone and give you a heart of flesh." As she claimed the Scripture, she felt a new and precious love stealing into her heart and became quite excited over what she thought was to be an instantaneous spiritual transformation. But then, in a vision, she saw a picture of her heart. It was like a wagon load of junk metal; dirty, rusted and useless. As she gazed at it in dismay, she saw one small piece of metal begin to glow and shimmer until it became like purest gold. The Holy Spirit witnessed to her that this was the transformation she had just experienced and that, as she continued to surrender to Him, little by little He would continue to make her heart new and pure.

The crucifixion of the old man, which begins with rebirth and is intensified by the baptism in the Holy Spirit, is a long and painful process. They may be right who claim that this purging is the "fire" John the Baptist spoke of when he said Jesus would baptize with the Holy Spirit and with *fire* (Luke 3:16). We would be less than honest to claim that such an inflow of spiritual power has no crucifying element within it. It has! But the joy of being in the Vine enables us to endure the pruning of the Vinedresser.

3. *Baptism in the Holy Spirit brings the Scriptures to life*.
The average adult church member seems to find Bible study about as pleasant as poison ivy. As a child he may have been forced to study Scripture in Sunday School,

but usually only until he was old enough to wear down his parent's resistance and drop out. Choose any church you like and chances are you'll find only a small handful of the adult members who are engaged in any real study of the Scripture. It's not that Mr. Average Christian has anything against the Bible. Ask him if he believes the Bible and he'll probably say yes. But he is indifferent toward it; it has no real claim on him. Obviously, what is lacking is Divine motivation, and that motivation is supplied through the baptism in the Holy Spirit. Christians receiving the baptism in the Holy Spirit find the Bible rising to towering heights as the Spirit creates a new hunger for the Word of God.

I received the baptism in the Spirit while studying for the ministry, and I already had more than a casual acquaintance with the Scriptures. But suddenly its message came alive as I began to find its characters were Spirit-filled or Spirit-led and were involved with a Living God. The whole Bible emerged as a living record of God's *supernatural* dealings with His children. The Holy Spirit—with blazing authority and power—revealed to me a major thesis in Scripture which the church today seems consistently to ignore: *What man cannot do for himself, God's loving, supernatural power will do for him, if he asks, believes, and obeys.* "Therefore the Lord waits to be gracious to you; therefore he exalts himself to show mercy to you" (Isaiah 30:18). With the Scriptures confronting me in this powerful new way, all desire to criticize, rationalize or quarrel with their authority began to melt away, and the Bible became the living Word of God to me.

Under the illumination of the Holy Spirit, the Biblical message becomes personal and intimate in a most remarkable fashion. At times, guidance and insight come

66

leaping from its pages in an almost supernatural way, answering particular questions and providing needed wisdom. Understandably, this kind of guidance is of such a personal, subjective nature that the full impact of its relevance is seldom communicable or applicable to a larger group. But the reliability of such guidance was established for me years ago, and I have come to trust this method of the Holy Spirit's working in my life implicitly.

4. *Baptism in the Holy Spirit makes God's guidance possible in new and powerful ways.*

Sometimes, overriding what we call common sense, the Holy Spirit will lead us into unexpected actions and decisions where we may feel frustrated and helpless until the results reveal a Will and Wisdom far beyond our own at work.

Once, while I was pastoring in Sharon, Pennsylvania, a Spirit-filled friend, Dr. Victor Dawe, and I drove to Pittsburgh to see Reverend Harald Bredesen. Harald, a close personal friend and prominent figure in the charismatic revival, was holding an informal seminar with some faculty and students at Duquesne University who were involved in the charismatic movement.

Both Victor Dawe and I had other matters to discuss with Harald and planned to arrive well before the meeting began. But entering Pittsburgh, we found ourselves ensnarled in maddening traffic and threading our way through a bewildering maze of road construction and unfinished expressways, none of which seemed to point in the direction of Duquesne University. Growing tired and irritable, we were tempted, several times, to give up the whole venture and return home. The time for the meeting arrived and we were nowhere near the University. Then, to make matters worse, we found ourselves on an expressway leading past the University but with no exit onto the campus, making it necessary to drive several miles before we could leave the expressway, turn around and make our way back. By this time, I was exasperated enough to regret I'd ever heard of the Christian faith in general and the charismatic movement in particular.

Finally, we found ourselves on the campus, and a helpful student gave directions to the building where the seminar was being held. It was now almost an hour past the scheduled time of meeting. As we pulled alongside the curb, we were relieved to find two adjacent parking spaces immediately in front of the entrance—the only two spaces in an otherwise unbroken line of parked cars. As I pulled into one space, a small sedan followed me into the second space. We climbed from the car and were astounded to see Harald Bredesen emerging from the other car.

Through circumstances unknown to us, he too had been delayed. While those responsible for the seminar scattered over the campus to gather the students and faculty who wished to meet Harald, Victor Dawe, Harald and I sat on the front steps and had a leisurely half-hour to discuss those things which were most important to us and to marvel how—in the midst of confusion and complaint—the Holy Spirit had worked to bring us together.

Other times, the Holy Spirit will move with urgency to get us into the will of God for a particular purpose. Several years ago, while serving a church in Toronto, Canada, I experienced such an incident. I was mowing the parsonage lawn one Saturday afternoon, when, under an unusual prompting of the Holy Spirit, I was moved to go attend a service at a healing revival being conducted in the west end of that city. On the way to the service, the Holy Spirit directed me to a hospital where one of my deacons lay recovering from surgery. As I approached the hospital, the Spirit revealed I would find the deacon near death and was to take his name to the healing service, request prayer for his healing, and stand in as his proxy for the laying on of hands. True to the Spirit's leading, I found the deacon near death, continued on to the healing service and stood in proxy for prayer and the laying on of hands in his behalf. God stayed the hand of death and the deacon recovered.

At times, this kind of prompting of the Holy Spirit seems so in conflict with our own natural desires, and at other times our plans seem so in conflict with His desires, that we are reluctant to yield in obedience. Often, the Holy Spirit must thwart our plans in order to make us receptive to His. This was true in the early church.

> And they went through the region of Phrygia and Galatia, having been forbidden by the Holy Spirit to speak the word in Asia. And when they had come opposite Mysia, *they attempted to go into Bithynia, but the Spirit of Jesus did not allow them*; so, passing by Mysia, they went down to Troas— Acts 16:6-8.

The Holy Spirit also gently teaches us that we alone are not responsible for the whole world. There are certain conditions and persons not in our personal "bundle" which—for reasons known only to God—are not in our province to help. A close study of the ministry of Jesus indicates He was subject to the discriminating guidance and direction of the Holy Spirit. While He loved all men and never refused to help or heal anyone who came seeking Him, still He did not force His ministry on people who were neither interested in Him nor ready to believe

His message. For example, when He visited the Bethesda pool where there lay a whole crowd of sick people, He was led by the Holy Spirit to minister only to one man (see John 5:1-9.)

5. *Baptism in the Holy Spirit gives more power in prayer*.

The church as a whole seems still asleep to the fact that earnest, believing prayer is the channel through which the miracle-working power of God flows. Many church members, and ministers as well, freely admit that petitionary or intercessory prayer has no place in their lives. I remember the shock and dismay I felt when I heard the admission of a seminary professor, who was an ex-navy chaplain and an ordained minister in my own denomination, frankly confess that he'd never in all his life seen anything happen, either to him or to anyone else, that would give him any assurance that God heard and answered prayer. Early in our spiritual journey, my wife and I began to experience definite and sometimes dramatic answers to prayer. It is still a matter of deep concern with us how few Christians avail themselves of this powerful weapon. After twenty years of trusting Him, we couldn't begin to count the times God has lovingly and graciously answered our petitions.

Just yesterday we experienced His love and bounty in this way. For several days we had been holding before Him a pressing financial obligation which totaled $94.28. We simply had no money with which to pay this obligation and knew of no source where such a sum would be forthcoming within the immediate future. Nevertheless, we prayed, trusting God, reminding Him of His promise to us that as long as we faithfully sought to minister in accordance with His will, He would provide for our needs. Then, in yesterday's mail came two checks from completely unexpected sources which totaled $95.00, and we rejoice, not only in God meeting our need, but in doing it with so exact an amount that there could be no question that He was a loving Father answering a specific request made by His children.

Thus, we see that Jesus' statements about prayer's power are not simply "flashes of brilliant hyperbole," as one Biblical critic rationalized, but instead are firm declarations of what God can and will do in response to believing, trusting prayer.

And the baptism in the Holy Spirit clearly adds a deeper dimension to prayer. The ability to pray in tongues brings with it a new spiritual freedom and creates a precious intimacy with Jesus not previously known. When uncertain how to pray in a given situation, the Spirit-filled Christian may slip over into praying in tongues with the confidence that such Spirit-directed prayer is more effective than his own intellectually-guided efforts. As Paul reminds us:

> Likewise the Spirit helps us in our weakness; *for we do not know how to pray as we ought,* but the Spirit himself intercedes for us with sighs too deep for words. And he who searches the hearts of men knows what is the mind of the Spirit, because the Spirit intercedes for the saints according to the will of God—Romans 8:26-27.

6. *Baptism in the Holy Spirit opens our eyes to the reality of Satan and his power.*

Baptism in the Holy Spirit opens the Christian's eyes, not only to the supernatural realities of God, but to the dominion of demons as well. The battle lines between good and evil, between God and Satan, are much more clearly drawn. Satan is no figment of an overactive imagination to be explained away by religious sophisticates. He is—as Jesus knew him to be—a personal adversary, real and cunning.

In Matthew 4:1-11, we have the account of Jesus' own temptation by the devil at the beginning of His ministry. The temptations were subtle and powerful, offered in terms of Jesus' special powers, tempting Him to achieve a quick and easy victory. Jesus met and overcame the tempter by a reliance on the Word of God. While the encounter was obviously a deeply personal and private experience, nevertheless it found its way into our New Testament because Jesus shared it with His disciples and so with us, that we might know and be warned of Satan's disruptive ministry.

The Scriptures clearly reveal that our sin, illness, poverty and fear are all the result of Satan's oppression. Jesus never once told anybody that sickness was from God; He recognized it and treated it for what it is, an affliction from the devil, to be cast out and destroyed by the power of the Holy Spirit. "The thief comes only to steal and kill and destroy; I came that they may have life, and have it abundantly" (John 10:10). "... God anointed Jesus of Nazareth with the Holy Spirit and with power... he went about doing good and healing all that were oppressed of the devil, for God was with him" (Acts 10:38). "The reason the Son of God appeared was to destroy the works of the devil" (1 John 3:8).

Paul tells us,

For we are not contending against flesh and blood, but against the principalities, against the powers, against the world rulers of this present darkness, against the spiritual hosts of wickedness in the heavenly places—Ephesians 6:12.

One of the amazing ministries Spirit-filled Christians are finding themselves engaged in is that of casting out demons. We have discovered that many forms of illness, both physical and mental, are the direct result of demonic oppression and that in such cases deliverance lies, not in the prayer of faith, but in taking authority over the demons in Jesus' name and commanding them to come out. The results are often quite remarkable.

In many cases, the demons manifest themselves in the person, just as they did in New Testament times, by taking over and speaking through the individual. They may argue or cajole or plead or insist on their right to be in the person. In the beginning they may refuse to come out and may curse or threaten the one taking authority over them. On command, they must name themselves, and the name usually reveals their sphere of activity.

While engaged in this ministry, I have personally confronted demons who gave such names as Pride, Hatred, Lies, Murder, Anger, Misery, Resentment, Loneliness, Laziness, Silliness, Gluttony, Self-destruction, Meanness, Madness, Lust, Infirmity, Blindness, Dumbness, Self-Pity, Thievery, Wantonness, Blasphemy, Shyness, Profanity, Vanity and many others.

Often, many demons may reside in a single personality, as in the case of Mary Magdalene in the New Testament out of whom Jesus cast seven demons (see Mark 16:9). In such cases, the demons may be expelled quickly, or the deliverance may take several hours or several prayer sessions until all of the demons are identified and cast out. Jesus Himself said that in some of these cases prayer and fasting is essential to being used in the deliverance ministry (Matthew 17:21).

We should also stress that it is one thing to cast the demons out and another to keep them out. To remain free, a person must stay vigilant in prayer and faithfully build up his spiritual resources. He must resist with real determination every effort of Satan to regain entry into his life.

This is not a casual ministry and should be undertaken only under the leading of the Holy Spirit and then only with much prayer and continual pleading of the blood of Christ for protection. Neither is it a ministry to be attempted alone since it can be quite physically exhausting. At times, physical help is needed in restraining the possessed person since the demons within may seek to cause bodily harm by throwing the person on the floor or banging his head against the wall. Therefore, the ministry should be undertaken only in teams of two or more.

Once the Spirit-filled Christian enters this spiritual arena and begins to battle Satan on his own ground, he must remain doubly on guard against the harassment and attacks of Satan upon his own person and other members of his family. Yet, when one is led into this ministry, he can approach it with determination and faith, knowing that Satan is a defeated foe and that he and his demonic underlings must give way before the authority and power of Jesus Christ.

7. *Baptism in the Holy Spirit brings a concern for the salvation of others.*

With the baptism in the Holy Spirit comes a new revelation of the ache in God's heart for the saving of His children. The Spirit-filled Christian begins to feel some of the compassion Christ felt when He wept over Jerusalem. "O Jerusalem, Jerusalem, killing the prophets and stoning those who are sent to you! How often would I have gathered your children together as a hen gathers her brood under her wings, and you would not" (Matthew 23:37).

This deep, compassionate yearning which the Holy Spirit shares with us is, of course, the basic motivation for Christian evangelism. The Bible plainly teaches that man is lost without Christ. "For the Son of man came to seek and to save the lost" (Luke 19:10). The term "lost" is God's term, not ours. He considers us His lost children until we are saved by the grace of Jesus Christ. The word "lost" is one of the most moving words in the English language. It signifies separation from all that is loved and familiar. Someone loved and cherished is missing. The word implies a fallen estate, separation from blessed security and privilege. If something is lost, it means it once was owned, once belonged to someone. If a child is lost, it means he's strayed beyond the protection of his parents. He faces danger and suffering which were never intended, and this means heartbreak and anguish for the parents who love him and who would move heaven and earth to get him back.

The story of the prodigal son in Luke 15 reveals more clearly than any other scripture the longing of God for the return of His lost children. The key verse is verse 20. The prodigal has squandered his inheritance and decides to return home. "And he arose and came to his father. *But while he was yet at a distance, his father saw him* and had compassion, and ran and embraced him and kissed him." There was only one reason why the Father had seen his son returning while he was still far away from the house; he had never stopped watching for his son's return. And when at last he identifies the gaunt, penitent figure of his son wearying into view, he rushes to meet him. "For this my son was dead, and is alive again; he was lost, and is found" (Luke 15:24). This, the Holy Spirit reveals, is the Father heart of God, longing for the saving of His lost children. And a measure of that great longing, by the Holy Spirit's quickening presence, becomes ours as well.

8. *Baptism in the Holy Spirit glorifies Jesus Christ.*

For many church members the Lordship of Christ is a puzzling and often fuzzy subject, and His place in their religion is not clearly defined. They are unsure and confused about Him. There is a direct relationship between the baptism in the Holy Spirit and accepting fully the Lordship of Christ. Indeed, it takes the Holy Spirit to reveal to us the full wonder and glory of Jesus, for as Jesus Himself said, "He (the Holy Spirit) will glorify me, for he will take what is mine and declare it to you" (John 16:14). Without the inward witness which comes with the baptism in the Holy Spirit, many people in the church consider Jesus as teacher, friend, guide, elder brother, example, leader or any one of a whole list of additional titles which, while showing respect, leave Him less than God. But under the tutelage of the Holy Spirit, the Spirit-baptized Christian is swept into a dazzling awareness of Jesus' Lordship. Like the early Christians, we become satisfied that He is God Incarnate. He is King of kings and Lord of lords! We accept at face value His own claim, "All authority in heaven and on earth has been given to me" (Matthew 28:18). We say, "Amen!" to Paul's statement, "For in him the whole fulness of deity dwells bodily" (Colossians 2:9).

Certainly, I loved Jesus before receiving the baptism in the Holy Spirit. I had accepted Him as my Lord and Savior before. Yet, He was my Lord with reservations because I loved Him with reservations. But after being baptized in the Holy Spirit, I came to understand why He

' been the all consuming passion in the lives of the early Christians because something akin to that passion began to burn within me. I know now what Paul meant in his wildly glorious statement of abandonment of self for the sake of Jesus Christ; "But whatever gain I had, I counted as loss for the sake of Christ. Indeed I count everything as loss because of the surpassing worth of knowing Christ Jesus my Lord" (Philippians 3:7-8).

9. *Baptism in the Holy Spirit reveals the depth of God's love.*

Miraculous though it seems, with the baptism in the Holy Spirit there begins to dawn on us the realization that our Heavenly Father loves each of us—unworthy as we are—with the same boundless love He bestowed upon His only begotten Son. Jesus was not only sustained by this love but prayed that it be revealed to us as well.

> I do not pray for these only, but also for those who believe in me through their word, that they may all be one. . . . I in them and thou in me, that they may become perfectly one, so that the world may know that thou has sent me *and hast loved them even as thou hast loved me*—(John 17:20, 23).

We are well aware how deep love between husband and wife or parents and children creates an environment conducive to a happy, satisfying life. And God's love for us, infinitely greater than our love for one another, revealed and experienced through the Holy Spirit, has far greater potential for transforming life. As we pray in the Spirit, there comes a sense of wonder at being tenderly surrounded and upheld by His love. Sometimes this spiritual union, in high moments of worship, becomes blissful almost beyond description. It is like a foretaste of heaven.

A number of years ago, several of us were gathered for Spirit-filled prayer in the home of Mrs. Toler Tucker of Raleigh, North Carolina, where we were overwhelmed by the presence of Jesus in the manner described above. During those rapturous moments, the Lord spoke in prophecy through a dear friend, Sister Mittie Watters, that the holy love we were experiencing was but a foretaste of what all Christians would experience when Jesus returned to reign in glory. In those moments, we seemed to occupy a special, secret place in the bosom of God. We knew the "security of the beloved."

Yet, this is not something selfish, to be appropriated by the very few. Rather, it is God's promise to everyone who will believe. Enveloped in this love, we know what it is to be safe, or "saved." We know what it is to be at peace with God. Jesus said, "My peace I give to you; not as the world gives..." (John 14:27).

Nothing this world offers can match that love. Remember the old hymn, "Blessed Assurance, Jesus is Mine"? This is it—the assurance that we are the beloved of God, eternally safe and secure. There are no adequate words here. Those who have begun to experience it know what we mean; those who have not, we pray will soon discover it for themselves.

PART II

Questions about speaking in tongues

CHAPTER 18

What is the evidence of the baptism in the Holy Spirit?

The only clear *scriptural* evidence of the baptism in the Holy Spirit is speaking in tongues. The first Christians to be baptized in the Holy Spirit were the 120 gathered in the upper room at Pentecost. The unique evidence that the 120 received the Holy Spirit was that "they began to speak in other tongues" (Acts 2:4). All the other spiritual gifts, such as healing and prophecy, appear in the Old Testament and in the Gospels. But with the descent of the Holy Spirit at Pentecost, which signified God's Presence in the disciples' lives in a new dimension, God gave a new gift: the gift of tongues.

The book of Acts records five separate occasions when the Holy Spirit was received. On three of these occasions, speaking in tongues is specifically mentioned as the visible sign accompanying the experience: at Pentecost (Acts 2:4), at the house of Cornelius (Acts 10:44-46), and at Ephesus (Acts 19:6). Paul received the Holy Spirit when Ananias laid hands on him and prayed (Acts 9:17), and, while tongues are not mentioned at that point, we know they were a part of Paul's spiritual experience by his own testimony: "I thank God that I speak in tongues more than you all" (1 Corinthians 14:18). The fifth occasion was the receiving of the Holy Spirit in Samaria (Acts 8:14-17). Philip had made converts, and the apostles at

Jerusalem sent down Peter and John to pray for their baptism in the Holy Spirit. While tongues are not directly identified in the account here, there was some *visible* evidence which made Simon the magician want to purchase from the apostles the ability to transmit the Holy Spirit. Many Biblical authorities agree that what Simon saw must have included speaking in tongues.

Then, there is the statement of Jesus in Mark 16:17-18 where tongues are listed along with other supernatural manifestations which were to follow the ministry of believers.

> And these signs will accompany those who believe: in my name they will cast out demons; *they will speak in new tongues* ... they will lay their hands on the sick, and they will recover.

So, according to Scripture, the identifying evidence or sign of receiving the baptism in the Holy Spirit is that of speaking in tongues. While there may be, and frequently are, other spiritual manifestations which accompany the experience of receiving the Holy Spirit, speaking in tongues remains the primary *initial* evidence.

CHAPTER 19

Can I receive the baptism in the Holy Spirit without speaking in tongues?

"With God all things are possible" (Matthew 19:26), therefore, the answer to this question is yes. However, it is a highly qualified yes! I personally know two people who received the baptism in the Holy Spirit in English rather than with unknown tongues. Both were exceptionally sensitive, prophetic men, true spiritual giants of our time. One is Dr. Frank Laubach, through whom the Holy Spirit manifested Himself supernaturally in English. The other was Rufus Moseley who, some months after his baptism in the Holy Spirit, began to speak in tongues and continued to witness faithfully to their value until his death. In a booklet entitled, "How To Enter, Abide, and Increase in Union With Jesus Christ," he makes this excellent statement: ·

> My feeling is that we must not be dogmatic and say that no one can have the baptism of the Holy Spirit unless he speaks in tongues. God, of course, can speak in English and in every tongue of men and angels. But He now seems a little more real to me when He speaks in tongues, especially if I am given the meaning of what is spoken. And when an ignorant person speaks in languages entirely

unknown to him, it is easy to see that he is not doing the speaking.

The Lord will do wonders for us even if we are prejudiced against tongues, if we are willing to yield at other points. He uses well the all of us that is yielded to Him while he waits for all that is not yielded to be yielded. He doesn't cut us off because we are not yielded at every point, but I have an idea that those of us who have been prejudiced against tongues will be faced around and will like them best of all (p. 41).

So, we must admit that the baptism in the Holy Spirit can be received without the manifestation of tongues, but we encourage no one to seek the baptism without expecting tongues. Both our understanding of spiritual gifts and our willingness to receive them affect what gifts and manifestations will appear. *Something is missing in your spiritual life if you have received the Holy Spirit yet have not spoken in tongues*. Those Spirit-filled Christians who have not yet spoken in tongues will receive a precious added assurance of God's presence and power when they do.

True, speaking in tongues is controversial, but if we are really seeking all God wants to bestow, we must seek God's blessings on God's terms, not ours. It is better to hold to the scriptural pattern than be swayed by human prejudices. All who speak in tongues have the authority of Scripture behind their experience. They do not need to defend their baptism in the Holy Spirit by saying, "Yes, I have received the baptism...BUT...I do not speak in tongues." So, if you tell me you have received the Holy Spirit without speaking in tongues, I do not deny your claim. But when you witness to me that you do speak in tongues, I rejoice because your experience is fully consistent with Scripture.

We encourage everyone seeking to be filled with the Holy Spirit to *seek the baptism on scriptural terms*, fully expecting to speak in tongues when they receive.

Those who ask the question, "Do I *have* to speak in tongues?" make it sound as if they are being asked to swallow an unpleasant dose of medicine. Their question indicates they believe tongues is something to be endured rather than enjoyed! Speaking in tongues is a blessed experience! It is a joy and a privilege to be able to communicate with the Lord in this new and exciting manner. Someone has rightly said, "You don't *have* to speak in tongues, you *get* to!" Or, as Dr. David du Plessis comments, "You don't have to, but you will."

Any person receiving the baptism in the Holy Spirit *can*, from the moment he accepts the Holy Spirit into his life in this new and powerful way, speak in tongues. The actual physical process is discussed elsewhere in this book. But rest assured that anyone filled with the Holy Spirit *can* speak in tongues.

Sometimes, one receiving the baptism may refuse— because of shyness or fear or false teaching—to yield his tongue and lips at the moment he receives the Spirit and so is robbed of this blessing for days or even weeks. But time and again, we have heard the testimony of such persons upon eventually yielding and receiving tongues. They admit that had they not resisted or backed away, they would have spoken in tongues the moment they received the baptism in the Holy Spirit.

CHAPTER 20

What is "speaking in tongues"?

Speaking or praying in tongues is a form of prayer in which the Christian yields himself to the Holy Spirit and receives from the Spirit a supernatural language with which to praise God. It is a miraculous manifestation of God's power, but one which combines both human and divine elements and which expresses both human and divine initiative. It is truly a cooperation between the Christian and the Holy Spirit.

Many people misunderstand what takes place when they hear someone praying or speaking in tongues. They are apprehensive over what might happen to them if they "let themselves go like that" or "let some other power take over." They assume the person is completely passive and that the Holy Spirit is doing it all. This is a completely erroneous impression of what is taking place. The person himself is very actively participating in the experience. As someone bluntly put it, "Without the Holy Spirit you can't, but without you the Holy Spirit won't."

Stated in the simplest way: Man does the speaking while the Holy Spirit furnishes the words. Acts 2:4 says, "They were all filled with the Holy Spirit and began to speak in other tongues, as the Spirit gave them utterance." A free translation might read, "they ... began to speak as the Spirit gave them words to say."

Speaking in tongues is a way of praying which liberates the spirit within and strengthens the Christian in a wonderful manner. The primary purpose of it is for use in one's own devotional life. Careful restrictions are placed upon its public use (see 1 Corinthians 14:18-19, 27-28).

Further information and instruction are given in Question No. 36 on *How Can I Receive the Baptism In The Holy Spirit?*, pages 134 to 143.

CHAPTER 21

Don't the Scriptures, "Do all speak with tongues?" (1 Corinthians 12:30) and "If any speak in tongues, let there be only two or at most three..." (1 Corinthians 14:27) indicate that not all Christians are meant to speak in tongues?

Certainly this has been used as an extensive argument by those who oppose speaking in tongues. In fact, many use Paul's statement, "let only two or three speak," not to *limit* tongues but to *prohibit* them entirely. Both these Scriptures must be considered in any discussion of tongues, but only in connection with Paul's statement in 1 Corinthians 14:5: "Now I want you all to speak in tongues..." How do we reconcile, "let there be only two or at most three..." and "I want you *all* to speak..."? Is Paul contradicting himself? No.

The confusion is cleared away when we consider the two sets of circumstances in which speaking in tongues appear in the New Testament. They appear both as a *sign* and as a *gift*. They appear as a *sign* or outward evidence which accompanies the baptism in the Holy Spirit in Acts 2:4, Acts 10:45-46, Acts 19:6, and Mark 16:17. They appear as a *gift* in Paul's references in 1 Corinthians 12 and 14.

Now in Acts, where tongues appear as a *sign*, all who received the baptism in the Holy Spirit spoke in tongues.

No limitation or restriction is placed on the manifestation, nor is there any suggestion that some received tongues while others did not. Nor is there any attempt to teach or instruct the recipients in the "proper use" of tongues. Speaking in tongues came to all, serving as the *sign* or evidence of the Holy Spirit's arrival in power upon them. I believe it is safe and correct to say that there is no such thing as misuse of tongues when they initially appear, at the time of one's receiving the baptism in the Holy Spirit.

But in 1 Corinthians, chapters 12-14, we find Paul discussing speaking in tongues as a *gift* among other gifts, to be used in the services of the church, only as the Holy Spirit directs, for "the common good" (1 Corinthians 12:7). Here Paul treats speaking in tongues, not in terms of *receiving*, but in terms of *exercising* the ability at a given time in the service of worship. He was explaining to those who had received the *sign* tongue when they were baptized in the Holy Spirit, and who could now manifest this ability to praise God in other languages, how, *in church*, any manifestation of tongues should fall in the same category as other manifestations of the Spirit such as prophecy, the word of wisdom, etc. Paul makes it clear that *in church*, if some individual is moved by the Holy Spirit to manifest tongues, it should be accompanied by the gift of interpretation so that the whole worshiping assembly may benefit by it (1 Corinthians 14:27). Yet, even here, Paul qualifies his statement by adding that prayer in tongues *without interpretation*, i.e., the sign tongue, may also be exercised during the church service, but only *silently*, so as not to disturb or disrupt the public worship service (1 Corinthians 14:28).

Certainly, in regard to speaking in tongues aloud, in church, with the gift of interpretation to follow, the question, "Do all speak with tongues?" must be answered with an emphatic No!

However, when we encourage those seeking the baptism in the Holy Spirit to seek it in terms of the initial scriptural evidence of speaking in tongues, we do not assume that all receiving tongues will be led by the Spirit to manifest the gift in a public worship service. Experience indicates that only a small percentage of those who manifest speaking in tongues at the time they receive the baptism in the Holy Spirit will ever be used for a public manifestation of tongues and interpretation in church. By far the most common use of tongues is during one's own private prayer time.

Essentially, what we have said here is: the accounts in the book of Acts show how the baptism in the Holy Spirit with speaking in tongues is received, while much of Paul's instructions in 1 Corinthians show how speaking in tongues is to be properly used and controlled in services of the church.

CHAPTER 22

Why should I speak in tongues?

The most obvious answer to this question is that the Scriptures encourage it. Jesus said it was one of the signs which was to follow the ministry of Christians; "And these signs will accompany those who believe ... they will speak in new tongues..." (Mark 16:17). And Paul, while recognizing the need for propriety in the public manifestation of tongues, nevertheless urges Christians to receive and make use of this significant gift. "Earnestly desire the spiritual gifts.... Now I want you all to speak in tongues.... I thank God that I speak in tongues more than you all..." (1 Corinthians 14:1, 5, 18). As the late Reverend Samuel Shoemaker observed, "The Christian needs every gift God offers."

The willingness to yield our tongues to God may also indicate a more profound surrender than almost any other act. The tongue is the primary instrument of expression of the human personality, and until God has dominion over the tongue, His control over us is relatively slight.

So the tongue is a little member and boasts of great things. How great a forest is set ablaze by a small fire! And the tongue is a fire. The tongue is an unrighteous world among our members, staining the whole body, setting on fire the cycle of nature, and set on fire by hell. For every kind of beast and bird, of reptile and sea creature, can be tamed and has been tamed by humankind, *but no human can tame the tongue*—a restless evil, full of deadly poison—James 3:5-8.

In addition, experience shows that prayer in tongues, which the Scriptures also refer to as "prayer in the Spirit" (see 1 Corinthians 14:14-15, Ephesians 6:18), enables us to pray with an ability and authority not our own. We do not always know how to pray in a given situation, but, holding the need up to the Father, we pray in tongues, knowing that our prayers are guided by the Holy Spirit.

When we cry, "Abba! Father!" it is the Spirit himself bearing witness with our spirit that we are children of God.... Likewise the Spirit helps us in our weakness; for we do not know how to pray as we ought, but the Spirit himself intercedes for us with sighs too deep for words. And he who searches the hearts of men knows what the mind of the Spirit is, because the Spirit intercedes for the saints according to the will of God—Romans 8:15-16, 26-27.

Why speak in tongues? Because it grants the Christian a freedom in prayer which enables him to praise God extravagantly, beyond the limiting confines of known speech. Our Lord had nothing but praise for those who worshiped Him extravagantly or served or trusted him extravagantly; the poor widow who gave God all the money she had (Luke 21:1-4), the Roman centurion and his tremendous faith in Jesus' healing power (Matthew

8:5-13) and Mary, who was extravagant in her devotion in anointing Him with precious ointment (John 12:3). Yet, many of us are so stingy and pinched in our relationship with God that any real freedom in prayer or worship is beyond us. Such freedom can come through praying in tongues.

It may help also to realize that there are strong Biblical reasons for speaking in tongues. Dr. Henry Ness, in his booklet "The Baptism With The Holy Spirit," lists twenty Bible reasons for speaking in tongues.

1. Speaking with tongues as the Holy Spirit gives the utterance is the *unique* spiritual gift identified with the Church of Jesus Christ. Prior to the day of Pentecost, all other gifts, 'miracles, and spiritual manifestations had been in evidence during the Old Testament times. On the Day of Pentecost, this new phenomenon came into evidence and became uniquely identified with the Church (Acts 2:4 and 1 Corinthians, chapters 12-14).

2. Speaking with tongues was ordained by God for the Church (1 Corinthians 12:28, 14:21).

3. Speaking with tongues is a specific fulfillment of prophecy (Isaiah 28:11, 1 Corinthians 14:21, Joel 2:28-29, Acts 2:16-18).

4. Speaking with tongues is a sign OF the believer (John 7:38, 39, Mark 16:17).

5. Speaking with tongues is a sign TO the unbeliever (1 Corinthians 14:22).

6. Speaking with tongues is a proof of the resurrection and glorification of Jesus Christ (John 16:7, Acts 2:22-24, 32-33).

7. Speaking with tongues is an evidence of the baptism with the Holy Spirit (Acts 2:4; 10:45-46; 19:6).

8. Speaking with tongues is a means of preaching to men of other languages (Acts 2:6-11).

9. Speaking with tongues is a spiritual gift for self-edification (1 Corinthians 14:4).

10. Speaking with tongues is a spiritual gift for spiritual edification for the Church (1 Corinthians 14:5).

11. Speaking with tongues is a spiritual gift for communication with God in private worship (1 Corinthians 14:2).

12. Speaking with tongues is a means by which the Holy Spirit intercedes through us in prayer (Romans 8:26, 1 Corinthians 14:14).

13. Speaking with tongues is a spiritual gift for "singing in the Spirit" (1 Corinthians 14:15, Ephesians 5:18-19).

14. The apostle Paul was thankful to God for the privilege of speaking in tongues (1 Corinthians 14:18).

15. The Apostle Paul desired that all would speak with tongues (1 Corinthians 14:5).

16. Speaking with tongues is one of the gifts of the Spirit (1 Corinthians 12:10).

17. The Apostle Paul ordered that speaking with tongues should not be forbidden (1 Corinthians 14:39).

18. Isaiah prophetically refers to speaking with tongues as a "rest" (Isaiah 28:12, 1 Corinthians 14:21).

19. Isaiah prophetically refers to speaking with tongues as a "refreshing" (Isaiah 28:12, 1 Corinthians 14:21).

20. Speaking with tongues follows as a confirma-

tion of the Word of God when it is preached (Mark
16:17, 20).

CHAPTER 23

Some say that speaking in tongues is just gibberish resulting from over-emotionalism. Isn't there danger in getting mixed up in anything like that?

No, not unless you deliberately seek out a place where such goings on are encouraged. It is true that certain individuals and churches show more emotion in their worship than others. Some shout and some cry. But these displays we find disturbing mainly because of their contrast to the quiet way we worship. This doesn't mean that noise is wrong and silence is right; it merely means their ways are different from ours. We may think their worship noisy and unseemly while they consider our worship dead and lifeless. Church history shows that all great revivals have been marked by the presence of physical phenomena such as trembling, weeping, shouting, fainting, and even dancing. They are not necessarily the work of the Holy Spirit as much as they are human reactions to the working of the Holy Spirit.

Yet, we should recognize that the baptism in the Holy Spirit often brings with it such transforming power that the recipient may seem suddenly overwhelmed. He may praise God in a loud voice; he may lift his hands in an act of involuntary worship; or he may fall on his knees in humble thanksgiving. When the Holy Spirit descended at Pentecost, the disciples were somewhat less than reserved.

In fact, they behaved in such an unusual manner that when Peter rose to preach, he began his sermon with a defense of their behavior, assuring the crowds they were not drunk.

Some of us think *any* emotion in religion is too much. We worship God much as we serve him, with grave reservations. We equate reverence with silence and save our enthusiasm (a word which means "in God") and our shouts for football games and political rallies. We simply have not considered Christianity worth getting excited about. But the baptism in the Holy Spirit is an exciting experience. One young minister was so infused with joy when he received the Holy Spirit that conservative friends suggested darkly he should be "put away for a while."

"That's all right with me," he replied. "For I'd rather be locked up with what I have than running loose with what I had." Yet for most, the experience is one of quiet joy. There may be deep emotion present when praying in tongues but never any loss of "control." This kind of prayer, like any other, is completely subject to the control of the pray-er.

Some modern translations of the New Testament call speaking in tongues "ecstatic speech" which is an unfortunate and inaccurate translation. In his booklet, "Speaking In Tongues: A Gift For The Body of Christ," Reverend Larry Christenson makes this clear.

The terms "ecstatic utterance" or "tongues of ecstasy" are *never* used in the Bible in reference to a speaker in tongues. Those who *hear* a speaker in tongues are sometimes described as "ecstatic" or "amazed" (existanto, Acts 2:7, exestesan, Acts 10:45) but the speaker himself is *never* described in this way. These misleading terms occur frequently

97

in commentaries and even in versions of the Bible, but there is no basis for this in the Bible text itself. This seems to be an assumption of the commentators who perhaps had not had the experience, and are therefore at a disadvantage in describing the subjective aspects.

There is nothing in the nature of speaking in tongues which is per se "ecstatic." It is, as the Bible so accurately puts it, simply "a speaking." It has the same emotional potential (and the same possibility of self-control) as speech or prayer in one's native tongue. The terms "ecstatic utterance" and "tongues of ecstasy" should be abandoned in reference to speaking in tongues. We should use the terms the Bible uses: "speaking in tongues" or "praying in the spirit."[1]

The idea that one has to become "ecstatic" or go into a trance or "lose control" in order to receive the Holy Spirit or manifest His gifts is simply not true. While emotional excesses may be indulged in by certain fringe groups, the fact is that most people receiving the baptism in the Holy Spirit today receive it among people who worship in churches similar to their own and whose religious backgrounds are compatible with theirs. God does not require us to try and be some other kind of person than we are to be filled with His Spirit.

Almost without exception this kind of question comes from people who have not had the experience. It is only natural that they should defend their position by gathering as many objections as they can. Most persons

---

[1] Christenson, *Speaking in Tongues, A Gift For The Body of Christ,* Fountain Trust, pp. 22, 23.

who have received the Holy Spirit with speaking in tongues once held such views themselves. I did. But once you receive the baptism in the Holy Spirit, once you speak in tongues yourself, you will understand how unfounded the fears and objections are.

CHAPTER 24

Are the tongues spoken today ever in known languages like they were at Pentecost?

Yes. But let us make it clear that this is not a valid test of the authenticity of the experience. True, at Pentecost the tongues were heard and understood by men of various nationalities (Acts 2:7-11). However, when the Holy Spirit fell on the house of Cornelius (Acts 10:44-46) and they all began to speak in tongues, there is no indication that anyone understood the languages. Yet Peter observed, "These people have received the Holy Spirit *just as we have* . . ." (Acts 10:47). Later, when he reported this incident to the church leaders at Jerusalem he said:

> As I began to speak, *the Holy Spirit fell on them just as on us at the beginning.* And I remembered the word of the Lord, how he said, "John baptized with water, but you shall be baptized with the Holy Spirit." *If then God gave the same gift* to them as He gave to us when we believed in the Lord Jesus Christ, who was I that I could withstand God?— Acts 11:15-17.

While we don't know if the languages spoken on this occasion were recognizable as they had been at Pentecost, it is clear Peter did not judge the authenticity of the experience by this, but by the tongues themselves. Remember, Peter and the others at Pentecost had not understood the languages they were speaking. It was the multitude which gathered outside who heard, "each in his own language" (Acts 2:11).

So the validity of speaking in tongues is not dependent upon the tongues being in a known language. Indeed, one argument Paul uses in 1 Corinthians 14 for encouraging Christians to seek the gifts of interpretation and prophecy is that tongues are unintelligible unless there is interpretation, and that in the church's service of worship, prophecy is more beneficial than speaking in tongues. "For one who speaks in a tongue speaks not to men but to God for no one understands him, but he utters mysteries in the Spirit" (1 Corinthians 14:2).

While the primary use of tongues is for prayer and praise, the Lord does, on occasion, use it as a means of communicating with men, or at least to convince men of the supernatural nature of the experience by allowing believers who naturally speak only one language to praise Him freely in another. This is what happened at Pentecost.

The outpouring of tongues was not initiated as a multiple conversation between the disciples and the foreigners who gathered, nor as a deliberate attempt on the part of the disciples to preach. They were praising God in languages furnished by the Holy Spirit but unknown to them. That foreign-speaking Jews heard and understood the praises in their own language was, for the disciples, simply a miraculous by-product of their experience. While Peter was among those praising God in other tongues, when he stood up to preach to the assembled multitude he spoke in his own native tongue.

However, there are frequent cases today where the

tongues spoken by a Spirit-filled believer are in a language unknown to him but recognized by one listening. Such incidents do serve to prove the supernatural nature of the experience.

An Indian student in Washington D.C. shared with me this interesting story. A minister who opposed the work of Pentecostal missionaries in India wrote a pamphlet denouncing the experience of speaking in tongues and in it quoted a single phrase he had heard as "meaningless gibberish." Disciples of the writer took copies of the pamphlet to distribute them in various villages where the Pentecostal missionaries were at work. Standing in the center of a particular village, one pamphleteer began denouncing the Pentecostal experience. He read aloud the example of "gibberish" included in the pamphlet only to have a native push his way excitedly through the crowd and ask him to repeat the phrase. Examination proved the "gibberish" was actually a quote from Scripture, spoken in the peculiar dialect of this native who lived many miles away. The phrase being shouted in derision was "You have been purchased," a reference to 1 Corinthians 6:20.

While still in seminary, I heard the story of an American minister praying in tongues which visiting worshipers recognized as their own language: Chinese. But while the minister was using Chinese syllables, he was stringing them together in ways of unique beauty and originality, forming complex sentences of praise to God which the Chinese Christians themselves had never thought of using.

Episcopalian minister Dennis Bennett has a man in his church in Seattle, Washington, whose prayer language has been identified as Mandarin Chinese. Father Bennett described, in his parish newsletter of April 12, 1967, a most striking example of tongues proving to be a known language. He writes:

> A pastor in Oregon tells me of a young Japanese woman married to a young American in his congregation. The Japanese girl had never accepted Christ, but came to the altar of the church with her husband, he to worship God, she to pray to Buddha! Just recently, my friend tells me, as the couple knelt at the altar in his church, a woman next to them began to speak in tongues. The Japanese girl clutched her husband's arm: "Listen," she said. The woman next to them was speaking Japanese, and through her God said: "You have tried Buddha and he has not helped you; why don't you try Jesus Christ?" God addressed this Japanese girl by her full name, known to no one in this country, and certainly not to the woman speaking, who had no idea how she was being used. Not only that, but the Japanese girl told my pastor friend: "She was speaking high Japanese, the very formal language which we only use in our temples and places like that."

Many, many other illustrations of a like nature could be included here, but these should be sufficient for us to see that yes, speaking in tongues today can be in a known language. But again, let us stress that this fact in no way verifies the authenticity of speaking in tongues. It is still a miraculous gift of the Holy Spirit, even in the majority of cases where no one is present who can identify the language.

CHAPTER 25

Is the desire to speak in tongues uncontrollable?

This question presupposes a fear similar to that expressed in question No. 23, and a part of its answer is to be found there. So re-read the answer to that question. Through erroneous teaching, many people have been led to believe that the Holy Spirit "makes people do things they don't want to do." They seem to assume that the human will and personality are completely shoved aside, or that they are powerless in the grip of the Holy Spirit, and are quite surprised to learn how gentle the Holy Spirit is in His dealings with us.

Speaking in tongues is a method of prayer and praise, and the one doing the praying is as much in control of his speaking as he is when he is praying in English, i.e. he starts or stops at will and decides if and when he is to speak. The Scriptures make this obvious since Paul gives the Corinthian Christians clear instructions as to when and where to speak in tongues, advice which would have been useless unless the person himself has complete control.

> If any speak in a tongue, let there be only two or at most three, and each in turn; and let one interpret. But if there is no one to interpret, let each of them keep silence in church and speak to himself and to

God—1 Corinthians 14:27-28.

These verses make it plain that it is up to the person to decide whether he speaks or not and—if he decides to speak in tongues—whether or not it will be out loud or only to himself.

Therefore, we see the desire to speak in tongues is *never* uncontrollable.

CHAPTER 26

Do you know what you are saying when you speak in tongues?

No, not unless you are given the interpretation by the Holy Spirit. The "other tongues" which the 120 began to speak at Pentecost were unknown to them but recognizable to the amazed listeners who, according to Scripture, were devout Jews from "every nation under heaven."

> And they were amazed and wondered, saying, "Are not all these who are speaking Galileans? And how is it that we hear, each of us in his own native language?... we hear them telling in our own tongues the mighty works of God"—Acts 2:7-8, 11.

So, not only did the 120 not know the languages with which they were praising God, but the amazed listeners *knew* they didn't know what they were saying. For them, this was proof of the miraculous nature of the experience.

When we are worshiping in the Spirit or praying in tongues in our private devotions, there is generally no need for interpretation. This form of prayer is not exercised for the benefit of the intellect. Paul says, "For if I pray in a tongue, my spirit prays but my mind is unfruitful (1 Corinthians 14:14). The Holy Spirit knows the content of our prayer for He inspires it; there is no need for us to understand. It is enough to know that God does.

> Likewise the Spirit helps us in our weakness; for we do not know how to pray as we ought, but the Spirit himself intercedes for us with sighs too deep for words.... because the Spirit intercedes for the saints according to the will of God—Romans 8:26-27.

CHAPTER 27

Why hasn't the gift of tongues been mentioned in the great revivals of the past?

The gift of tongues has been prominent in some great revivals of the past, barely mentioned in some, and ignored or disparaged in others. In the great Pentecostal outpouring which began in the first decade of this century, speaking in tongues was the most talked-about and controversial feature in the revival. This revival, which caught fire in the famed Azusa Street Mission in Los Angeles in 1906, gave birth to a number of the strong Pentecostal denominations in our country today.

But there is real spiritual truth in the statement: "What we receive from God is determined by what we expect from Him." In many an earlier revival, though there were great manifestations of God's power, few people expected speaking in tongues to appear and few people saw them. Still, there are accounts of the revivals of John Wesley, Dwight Moody, Charles Finney and others which take note of speaking in tongues, although they never played a prominent part.

The *Encyclopedia Britannica* states that speaking in tongues has recurred in Christian revivals of every age. There is also evidence in the reports of some revivals that where speaking in tongues appeared, they were squelched as emotionalism—even though shouting, laughing, crying, dancing and trembling, even rolling on the floor were considered "genuine" signs of the Holy Spirit's working. It also seems apparent that speaking in tongues was in evidence in other revivals where singing and laughing in the Spirit were heard, but that the speaking in tongues simply passed unrecognized.

PART III

*Questions about receiving the baptism
in the Holy Spirit*

CHAPTER 28

If I receive the baptism in the Holy Spirit, will it lead me away from my own church?

No, not unless you let it. Twenty, even ten years ago, the chances would have been much greater that you would have felt compelled to change churches. Around the turn of the century, when the baptism in the Holy Spirit began to blaze up in the church, many persons receiving it found themselves ostracized from their own congregations. This very fact led to the establishment of many of the present-day Pentecostal denominations. Today, however, it is widely recognized that Pentecost is not a denomination but an experience; an experience of God's power which is being received by people in all denominations.

The spiritual climate in the church has changed greatly in recent years with individual congregations, even whole denominations, rapidly reversing themselves on the question of the baptism in the Holy Spirit. Today, the overall attitude of most denominations is much more open. Seldom does one feel compelled to leave his denomination or his local church.

It is true, however, that over-zealousness or over-eagerness in wanting to share your experience may tend to alienate you from some of your church friends. If you are to be a faithful witness to what God is doing in your life, a certain amount of this estangement seems inevitable. But a gentle witness, filled with love, plus a determined effort to avoid all evidence of spiritual pride, tends to meet little opposition. And the joy which this precious relationship with Jesus brings far outweighs any criticism which may come our way.

For additional comments on this subject turn to Question No. 37.

CHAPTER 29

Where do I find the baptism in the Holy Spirit in Scripture?

Just as the coming of Jesus was foretold by the Old Testament prophets hundreds of years before His birth, so was the baptism in the Holy Spirit prophesied long before Pentecost.

In Isaiah 28:11 we hear the prophet saying, "For with stammering lips and another tongue will he speak to this people" (*KJV*). Centuries later, as Paul writes under the anointing of the Holy Spirit to the Corinthians, he applies this scripture to speaking in tongues (1 Corinthians 14:21-22).

Again the prophet Isaiah anticipates the coming Pentecostal age with its baptism in the Holy Spirit when he prophesies,

> For I will pour water on the thirsty land, and streams on the dry ground; I will pour out my Spirit upon your descendants, and my blessing on your offspring—Isaiah 44:3.

Then the prophet Joel proclaims:

> And it shall come to pass afterward, that I will pour out my spirit on all flesh; your sons and your

daughters shall prophesy, your old men shall dream dreams, and your young men shall see visions. Even upon the menservants and maidservants in those days, I will pour out my spirit—Joel 2:28-29.

You will recall how, on the day of Pentecost, Peter stands to his feet and addresses the multitudes, claiming the phenomenon they have beheld (the disciples praising God in other tongues) is the fulfillment of Joel's prophecy (Acts 2:14-18).

Now these were all Old Testament prophecies which were spoken hundreds of years before Jesus' ministry on earth or the coming of Pentecost. But with the beginning of Jesus' earthly ministry, we find additional prophecies of the promised baptism in the Holy Spirit. They begin with John the Baptist:

> John answered them all, "I baptize you with water; but he who is mightier than I is coming, the thong of whose sandals I am not worthy to untie; he will baptize you with the Holy Spirit and with fire"— Luke 3:16.
> I myself did not know him; but he who sent me to baptize with water said to me, "He on whom you see the Spirit descend and remain, this is he who baptizes with the Holy Spirit"—John 1:33.

Then there are the words of Jesus Himself:

> "If anyone thirst, let him come to me and drink. He who believes in me, as the scripture has said, 'Out of his heart shall flow rivers of living water.'" Now this he said about the Spirit, which those who

116

believed in him were to receive; for as yet the Spirit had not been given, because Jesus was not yet glorified—John 7:37-39.

What father among you, if his son asks for a fish, will instead of a fish give him a serpent; or if he asks for an egg, will give him a scorpion? If you then, who are evil, know how to give good gifts to your children, how much more will the heavenly Father give the Holy Spirit to those who ask him!—Luke 11:11-13.

As Jesus' earthly ministry drew to a close and He met with the disciples for the last time in the upper room, His instructions to them were liberally laced with promises of the coming of the Holy Spirit.

And I will pray the Father, and he will give you another Counselor, to be with you for ever, even the Spirit of truth, whom the world cannot receive, because it neither sees him nor knows him; you know him, for he dwells with you, and will be in you—John 14:16-17.

These things I have spoken to you, while I am still with you. But the Counselor, the Holy Spirit, whom the Father will send in my name, he will teach you all things, and bring to your remembrance all that I have said to you—John 14:25-26.

But when the Counselor comes, whom I shall send you from the Father, even the Spirit of truth, who proceeds from the Father, he will bear witness to me—John 15:26.

Nevertheless I tell you the truth: it is to your advantage that I go away, for if I do not go away, the Counselor will not come to you; but if I go, I will send him to you. And when he comes, he will convince the world of sin and of righteousness and of judgment—John 16:7-8.

I have yet many things to say to you, but you cannot bear them now. When the Spirit of truth comes, he will guide you into all the truth; for he will not speak on his own authority, but whatever he hears he will speak, and he will declare to you the things which are to come. He will glorify me, for he will take what is mine and declare it to you—John 16:12-14.

Then after Jesus' death and resurrection and before his ascension, he gives his disciples repeated assurances of the coming of the Holy Spirit with power, even as He had promised:

And behold, I send the promise of my Father upon you; but stay in the city, until you are clothed with power from on high—Luke 24:49.

And while staying with them he charged them not to depart from Jerusalem, but to wait for the promise of the Father, which, he said, "you heard from me, for John baptized with water, but before many days you shall be baptized with the Holy Spirit."

So when they had come together, they asked him, "Lord, will you at this time restore the kingdom to Israel?" He said to them, "It is not for you to know times or seasons which the Father has fixed by his own authority. But you shall receive power when the Holy Spirit has come upon you; and you shall be my witnesses in Jerusalem and in Judea and Samaria and to the end of the earth"—Acts 1:4-8.

And these signs will accompany those who believe: in my name they will cast out demons; they will speak in new tongues . . . they will lay their hands on the sick, and they will recover—Mark 16:17.

It is significant to note that the very last statements Jesus made to his disciples before his ascension to the Father were about the power they were to receive from the baptism in the Holy Spirit (Acts 1:8) and the miraculous signs that were to follow their ministry (Mark 16:17).

In obedience to their Lord's command, the disciples returned to Jerusalem, took up their vigil in the upper room, and waited and prayed expectantly until the day of Pentecost. Then it happened.

When the day of Pentecost had come, they were all together in one place. And suddenly a sound came from heaven like the rush of a mighty wind, and it filled all the house where they were sitting. And there appeared to them tongues as of fire, distributed and resting on each one of them. And they were all filled with the Holy Spirit and began to speak in other tongues, as the Spirit gave them utterance—Acts 2:1-4.

Jesus had kept His word and had sent them "the promise of the Father," and the disciples received the baptism in the Holy Spirit with joy.

At this point in history, the baptism in the Holy Spirit was made available to every believer. "Repent, and be baptized every one of you in the name of Jesus Christ for the forgiveness of your sins; and you shall receive the gift of the Holy Spirit" (Acts 2:38). The age of the Holy Spirit had begun! We assume God made no mistakes and that He hasn't changed His mind about what He did. He did it right when He did it the first time. The disciples received the Holy Spirit, and the evidence that they received was that they spoke in other tongues. Pentecost gives us an historic pattern to go by. We know we have received the baptism in the Holy Spirit when our experience matches that of the 120 at Pentecost.

All the Scriptures quoted thus far pointed toward the event in Acts 2:4. But there are also Scriptures which record the baptism in the Holy Spirit *after* Pentecost.

Now when the apostles at Jerusalem heard that Samaria had received the word of God, they sent to them Peter and John, who came down and prayed for them that they might receive the Holy Spirit; for it had not yet fallen on any of them, but they had only been baptized in the name of the Lord Jesus. Then they laid their hands on them and they received the Holy Spirit—Acts 8:14-17.

So Ananias departed and entered the house. And laying his hands on him he said, "Brother Saul, the Lord Jesus who appeared to you on the road by which you came, has sent me that you may regain your sight and be filled with the Holy Spirit"—Acts 9:17.

While Peter was still saying this, the Holy Spirit fell

on all who heard the word. And the believers from among the circumcised who came (to the house of Cornelius) with Peter were amazed, because the gift of the Holy Spirit had been poured out even on the Gentiles. For they heard them speaking in tongues and extolling God—Acts 10:44-46.

While Apollos was at Corinth, Paul passed through the upper country and came to Ephesus. There he found some disciples. And he said to them, "Did you receive the Holy Spirit when you believed?" And they said, "No, we have never even heard that there is a Holy Spirit." And he said, "Into what then were you baptized?" They said, "Into John's baptism." And Paul said, "John baptized with the baptism of repentance, telling the people to believe in the one who was to come after him, that is, Jesus." On hearing this, they were baptized in the name of the Lord Jesus. And when Paul had laid his hands upon them, the Holy Spirit came on them; and they spoke with tongues and prophesied—Acts 19:1-6.

In addition to the Scriptures quoted here, chapters 12-14 of Paul's First Corinthian letter deal at length with the nine spiritual gifts which become available to the Christian, once he is baptized in the Holy Spirit.

CHAPTER 30

How can I become worthy to receive the baptism in the Holy Spirit?

You can't. There is no way to become worthy. The gift of the Holy Spirit, like the gift of salvation, cannot be earned; it can only be received by faith. It is not bestowed as a prize nor handed out like wages earned. If you could become good enough to earn it, you wouldn't need it! The idea that we earn God's gifts by our good behavior is a great stumbling block to receiving spiritual power today. The only righteousness available to you and me is the righteousness imputed to us *because of our faith in Jesus Christ.* "For we hold that a man is justified by faith apart from works of law" (Romans 3:28). The old heresy of salvation by works often rears its ugly head to rob the Christian of God's promised gifts. What Paul says about Israel is true of many well-meaning church members today who are relying on their good behavior to save them.

I bear them witness that they have a zeal for God, but it is not enlightened. For, being ignorant of the righteousness that comes from God, and seeking to establish their own, they did not submit to God's righteousness. For Christ is the end of the law, that every one who has faith may be justified—Romans 10:2-4.

It is not our good works but our faith in Jesus Christ which saves us. Redemption is ours, not by *trying*, but by *trusting*. In the same manner, it is by simple trust in God's promise, and not by striving to be "worthy," that we receive the baptism in the Holy Spirit. Sometimes, we hear people say, "Well, I'm just waiting until God decides to give me the Holy Spirit," or, "God will baptize me with the Holy Spirit when He decides I'm worthy." Such people could not be more mistaken! They are being robbed of God's blessing by their own ignorance. Baptism in the Holy Spirit is immediately available to all who humbly and sincerely ask in faith.

CHAPTER 31

What are the hindrances to receiving the baptism in the Holy Spirit?

Obviously, there are many hindrances if one is not in a right relationship with Jesus Christ. Unconfessed sin, unchristian attitudes or practices, involvement in religious cults that deny the divinity of Christ, fear, or an unforgiving spirit, all are severe hindrances. But I am assuming that this question comes from one who is a Christian in a right relationship with the Lord and who earnestly desires to receive the baptism in the Holy Spirit.

Experience shows that there are two major hindrances which block receptivity to the baptism in the Holy Spirit. The first is scriptural ignorance. For years the Biblical doctrine of the Holy Spirit has been glossed over or ignored by our ministers and Bible teachers. Most Christians are still in the dark concerning what the Bible says about the Holy Spirit and His power. Once the same amount of study and discussion has been given to the Scriptures dealing with the baptism in the Holy Spirit as the Scriptures dealing with baptism in water, we will have much more helpful literature on the subject. People will not ask for spiritual power they do not know exists. Many of us are still like the Ephesian disciples who told Paul, "No, we have never even heard that there is a Holy Spirit" (Acts 19:2). Today, with the increasing spread of the charismatic revival, we are witnessing a return to Biblical studies on the subject and a heartening decline in Biblical ignorance.

But years of wrong teaching and Biblical ignorance also leave a psychological barrier that creates difficulty in receiving the baptism, even after we are intellectually convinced it is real. We must cry out like the father of the epileptic boy, "I believe; help my unbelief!" (Mark 9:24).

The other major hindrance is fear of what others may think or say—fear of public opinion. Until we want the Holy Spirit more than we want the approval of our fellow church members; until we want the power of God more than we want respectability; until we are so spiritually hungry we don't really care what other people think, we may not find ourselves very receptive. Most of us have wanted God on our terms and have steadfastly refused to let Him have us on His terms. For this reason, we find it difficult to move into new spiritual experiences. Many people seem to have arrived at the conclusion that speaking in tongues is somehow improper for good, orthodox church members. Perhaps the basic question we need to ask ourselves is whether we want to be prim, proper and powerless, or faithful, yielded and powerful. It seems well-nigh impossible to be both.

CHAPTER 32

If the baptism in the Holy Spirit comes from God, shouldn't it be spontaneous? Why the necessity for instructions in how to receive?

We don't think it strange to help people in receiving Christ as Savior by outlining for them several "steps to salvation." How many millions of brochures and tracts do you suppose have been distributed on "How to be saved"? This doesn't mean that people earn salvation or that it is not a sovereign act of God's grace. Neither does it mean that people cannot find salvation while reading the Word of God alone, with no human help. But we do know that information can be furnished which will help the "inquirer" to accept Jesus Christ as Lord and Savior.

The same thing is true about the baptism in the Holy Spirit. If we were as unbiased in our thinking about the Holy Spirit as the first Christians were, perhaps there would be less need for instruction. But most of us have erroneous teaching and ingrown prejudice to overcome. So instructions are given to help undo false teaching and to make people more receptive to encounter Jesus as the baptizer in the Holy Spirit.

The Scriptures make it plain that in seeking the blessings of God *how* we ask is as important as what we ask for. Jesus gave instruction to the disciples in matters pertaining to prayer. And if we examine the Scriptures closely, we find evidence of Jesus teaching the disciples about the coming of the Holy Spirit. Even the experience of Pentecost may not have been as spontaneous as it first appears since Jesus may have told his disciples to expect the manifestation of tongues which came at Pentecost. Certainly, He mentioned tongues as one of the miraculous signs which would follow those who believed: "And these signs will follow those who believe: in my name they will cast out demons; *they will speak in new tongues . . .*" (Mark 16:17), and he made this statement just before His ascension, only ten days before Pentecost.

CHAPTER 33

Does one have to receive the laying on of hands to be baptized in the Holy Spirit?

There are five accounts in the book of Acts where people received the baptism in the Holy Spirit. In three of the five accounts, those who received were ministered to through the laying on of hands. In Acts, chapter 8, Peter and John are sent down to Samaria to pray for Philip's converts to receive the Holy Spirit. Acts 8:18 says that the Spirit was given through the laying on of hands. Then, in Acts 9, we read where Ananias comes to lay hands on Saul that he might receive his sight and "be filled with the Holy Spirit" (Acts 9:17). Thirdly, Acts 19 tells of Paul laying hands on the Ephesian disciples. "And when Paul had laid his hands upon them, the Holy Spirit came on them; and they spoke with tongues and prophesied" (Acts 19:6). So, the Scriptures make a good case for the practice of laying on of hands in connection with prayer for the baptism in the Holy Spirit.

If you desire the baptism in the Holy Spirit and seek out a church or prayer meeting where this ministry is offered, it is likely you will receive the laying on of hands in connection with the prayer. Receiving the Holy Spirit often seems easier when hands are laid on the head of the candidate as prayer is offered.

Yet, having said this, we must note that on the other

two occasions in the book of Acts—Acts 2, where the Spirit falls at Pentecost and in Acts 10 where Cornelius' household receives the Spirit—there was no laying on of hands.

Today, we see it happening both ways at the same time. In meetings where a number are seeking the Holy Spirit, we may pray one inclusive prayer for all and then begin ministering to the candidates individually, encouraging them and laying hands on their heads. But the Holy Spirit often moves well ahead of the laying on of hands, for we usually find a number receiving and praising God in tongues long before we get to them.

So, the only accurate way we can answer this question is to say that the laying on of hands for the receiving of the Holy Spirit is scriptural, often helpful, but not always necessary.

CHAPTER 34

How can I know that what I receive is the baptism in the Holy Spirit and not a counterfeit from Satan?

If you are sincere and honest in seeking a blessing from the Lord, you need have no fear of a counterfeit from Satan. If you ask God for the baptism in the Holy Spirit, then that's what you receive. We have Jesus' own word for it.

> What father among you, if his son asks for a fish, will instead of a fish give him a serpent; or if he asks for an egg, will give him a scorpion? If you then, who are evil, know how to give good gifts to your children, how much more will the heavenly Father give the Holy Spirit to those who ask him!—Luke 11:11-13.

What could be plainer than that? Jesus said that if the Father didn't keep His Word, He would be less than an evil man, for even an evil man knows how to give good gifts to his children.

The fear of a counterfeit is one of Satan's favorite tricks to discourage sincere Christians from seeking all God has for them. I cannot make the emphasis strong enough when I say, God's Word is to be trusted! Wholly. Completely. Implicitly. God *cannot* deny Himself. He *cannot* deny His own Word. If you ask for a blessing from God, He *cannot* respond with a counterfeit from Satan.

When this question arises—as it often does—in sessions where we are about to pray for people to receive the baptism, we answer in this way: "We're going to pray now that the Lord Jesus Christ will baptize every one of you in the Holy Spirit. We want each of you to accept—by faith—that from this point on everything that happens is of the Holy Spirit."

I've had the privilege of praying for many hundreds of people to receive the baptism in the Holy Spirit, and I've never yet seen anyone receive a counterfeit. And I don't believe I ever will.

CHAPTER 35

Where should I go to receive the baptism in the Holy Spirit?

No one place is better than any other. People have received the baptism in Pentecostal tent meetings, in all kinds of churches including the Episcopal and Roman Catholic, in prayer meetings, in homes, and in almost every conceivable circumstance. I know of a minister who received while preparing a sermon in his study; another who received while preaching to his congregation. I know Christians who have received while driving a car, while lying in bed, even while taking a bath. My own brother, a colonel in the Air Force, received the baptism in the Holy Spirit as we sat praying together in a parked station wagon on a deer ranch in South Texas.

Just a few months ago, my wife and I prayed two young men through to the baptism in the Holy Spirit in our own station wagon in Atlanta, Georgia, as they waited to catch a plane. The plane was delayed for three hours, and I believe God did it in order that time might be made available for us to counsel and pray with those men. Another young friend received the baptism while traveling with a touring choir in Italy. Strange as it seems, she received the Holy Spirit and began praising God quietly in tongues as she stood with several hundred other people in St. Peter's Cathedral in Rome, during an audience with the Pope.

You see, it isn't the *place* you're in that's important, it's the *state* you're in that counts. If you are trustfully and prayerfully seeking this deeper experience with God, it can happen anywhere.

But having shared these incidents, let me hasten to encourage you to seek fellowship in some church or some charismatic prayer group where you will find those who have the ministry of helping others to receive. It is most likely that right in your own town or neighborhood there is a church or a house prayer meeting with this ministry.

Yet, if you have difficulty in locating such a group, or if you are one of those shy people who are reluctant to have others pray over you or to receive the laying on of hands, then be assured that you can receive the baptism in the Holy Spirit alone. In fact, you can receive it before you lay this book down, if you will ask in faith and cooperate with the Holy Spirit. We are not meant to "tarry" or wait, we are meant to believe and receive. The following chapter offers specific steps which can be of help to you if you are ready—right now—to move into this wonderful new relationship with the Lord. Why stand ye here? Jesus is waiting to baptize with power!

CHAPTER 36

How can I receive the baptism in the Holy Spirit?

(Much of the material included in this answer is taken from chapter 20 of my book, FACE UP WITH A MIRACLE, published by Whitaker House.)

Toward the end of his account of our Lord's life, the apostle John said, "Now Jesus did many other signs in the presence of the disciples, which are not written in this book; but these are written that you may believe that Jesus is the Christ, the Son of God, *and that believing* you may have life in His name" (John 20:30-31). In something of the same manner, the questions and answers in this book have been shared "That you may believe that the risen, glorified Jesus is still baptizing in the Holy Spirit, *and that receiving* you may have supernatural power in His name."

The incidents listed in the preceding chapter make it clear that there is no single technique or method of preparation essential for receiving the baptism in the Holy Spirit. Let me hasten to say, however, that there is one prerequisite which is absolutely essential. *If you have not already done so, you must accept the Lord Jesus Christ as your personal Savior.* By no means should anyone who is not a believing Christian pray for the baptism in the Holy Spirit!

There are two basic ingredients involved in the baptism in the Holy Spirit: the readiness of our Lord Jesus to baptize the believer, and the desire and readiness of the Christian to receive the baptism. If you are ready to receive the baptism in the Holy Spirit, this chapter is especially for you. I suggest that first you read the entire chapter, then at your own appointed time, in the privacy of your prayer corner, reread the chapter, carefully following each outlined step until the promised baptism in the Holy Spirit with the miracle of praising God in a new language becomes your own joyous possession. Praise God, He is *faithful* and will not let your desire go unfulfilled. Are you ready?

1. *Find a time and place for quiet prayer and meditation.*
   While it helps to be in the presence of a group of Spirit-filled Christians who can instruct, encourage and pray with you, such a fellowship is not essential. You may receive in your own home. Just find a place where you can be quiet and undisturbed for a period of prayer and waiting upon the Lord. The physical surroundings are not important as long as you can be quiet and comfortable. You may sit or kneel or take whatever position that will encourage your sense of reverence and spiritual expectancy.

2. *Reread the Scriptures where the Holy Spirit is promised.*
   These scriptures are already written out for you in chapter 29, beginning on page 115. Reread them carefully, affirming that they apply to *you*. After you have reread those passages, I want to point you to a seemingly unrelated, but very important and helpful, passage of Scripture: Matthew 14:22-31.

   Then (Jesus) made the disciples get into the boat

and go before him to the other side, while he dismissed the crowds. And after he had dismissed the crowds, he went up into the hills by himself to pray. When evening came, he was there alone, but the boat by this time was many furlongs distant from the land, beaten by the waves; for the wind was against them. And in the fourth watch of the night he came to them, walking on the sea. But when the disciples saw him walking on the sea, they were terrified, saying, "It is a ghost!" And they cried out for fear. But immediately he spoke to them, saying, "Take heart, it is I; have no fear."

And Peter answered him, "Lord, if it is you, bid me come to you on the water." He said, "Come." So Peter got out of the boat and walked on the water and came to Jesus; but when he saw the wind, he was afraid, and beginning to sink he cried out, "Lord, save me." Jesus immediately reached out his hand and caught him, saying to him, "O man of little faith, why did you doubt?"

This Scripture contains the story of how Peter sought and experienced a miracle. It is significant for you, because to receive the baptism in the Holy Spirit and speak in tongues is to experience a miracle. By examining this story and identifying yourself with Peter and his actions, you can be greatly helped to receive.

When Peter saw Jesus approaching on the water he said, "*Lord, if it is you*, bid me come...." Peter wanted assurance that the miracle he sought was in accordance with the will of God for his life. Many people today ask, "How do I know it's God's will that I receive the baptism in the Holy Spirit?" The Scriptures you reread about the baptism make it abundantly clear that the Lord *does* desire to bestow this gift on every Christian. So accept His will for you in this matter with joy and anticipation, know that His invitation applies to "*you* and to your children and to *all* that are far off" (Acts 2:39).

Now let us also note that Peter said, "Lord, if it is you, *bid me come to you on the water*." Peter *knew* he was asking the Lord for a miracle, asking Him to provide what no man on earth could grant. Only God could provide, by His supernatural power, the means for Peter to walk on the water. By the same token, the baptism in the Holy Spirit and speaking in tongues is a miracle which no man on earth can grant. Only God, by His supernatural power, can fill you with His Holy Spirit and enable you to speak in tongues.

Jesus told Peter to "Come" because He knew God's power would sustain Peter on top of the water. Jesus tells you to "Receive" because He knows God's power will fill you and enable you to speak in tongues.

By his willingness to come in response to Jesus' invitation, Peter, in effect, was saying, "Lord, if You say I can do it—if You say I can walk on the water—I trust You to make it possible." So also, you who are seeking the baptism in the Holy Spirit must say, "Lord, if You say I can receive—if You say I can speak in tongues—I trust You to make it possible."

3. *Pray the prayer of invitation.*

In a simple, fervent prayer, ask Jesus to fill you with the Holy Spirit. You may use a prayer like the following:

"Lord Jesus Christ, I believe with all my heart that the baptism in the Holy Spirit is meant for me. Just as I trust You for my eternal salvation, so now do I trust You to give me Your Holy Spirit with the evidence of speaking in tongues. I now open my life to receive the fullness of Your

137

Holy Spirit within. Thank You, Lord Jesus, Amen."

4. *Receive the Holy Spirit within.*

Having prayed your prayer, believe and act on it. Know that at this very moment the Holy Spirit is moving into your life in a new and powerful way in answer to your prayer. Claim your answer! In a conscious act of surrender, let Him have full control of your body, mind and spirit. Be confidently aware of His presence within.

At this point, you may actually *feel* the presence of the Holy Spirit, physically. His presence may come as a warmth enveloping you, or as a silent powerful Presence enfolding you. You may experience a tingling sensation or a gentle vibration as if touched by an electric current. But even if you feel nothing, rest quietly in the confidence that the Holy Spirit is *now* coming upon you in power and is about to furnish you with a new language of prayer and praise to God.

5. *Receive and speak the language the Holy Spirit gives.*

This is the point where your faith and trust must resolve themselves into action. In the Biblical story of Peter's miracle, this is the point where Peter acted boldly and in faith, even as you must. The Scripture simply states, "So Peter *got out of the boat and walked . . .*" These few words hold the key! They reveal how the miracle took place, and when you understand this, you have in your hand the key to speaking in tongues.

Before the miracle of God could take place, Peter had to do his part. But Peter didn't do anything supernatural, he just stepped out of the boat and began to walk—just as he would have had the boat been pulled up on shore. It was an act of faith and courage, but it was a purely human act. Then, when Peter acted in faith, God moved supernaturally to perform the miracle. As Peter walked, God held the water firm under his feet. Read the story carefully. God didn't lift Peter out of the boat and float him across the waves. Peter walked naturally while God held him up supernaturally. If Peter had waited for the power of God to lift him out of the boat and float him across the waves to Jesus, he would still be in the boat today!

So it is with the miracle of speaking in tongues. The miracle is not *that* you speak; you do your own speaking just like Peter did his own walking. You are to step out with your own lips and voice, just as Peter stepped out with his own legs and feet. The miracle comes when, as you open your mouth to speak, you trust God to furnish you with a new language of praise—words and syllables in a new and unknown tongue. Peter walked—and trusted God to hold the water firm under his feet. You are to speak, trusting God to give you a new language with which to praise Him. Lift up your voice in faith, trusting that *as you begin to speak*, it will be in a new and beautiful language you have never heard before.

Do not hesitate. Do not be afraid to open your mouth and speak. Refusing to speak out in faith leaves you like Peter sitting in the boat. As long as he sat there and did nothing, there was no miracle. As long as you keep silent, there will be no miracle of speaking in tongues.

When the Holy Spirit fell at Pentecost (Acts 2:4) "... they were all filled with the Holy Spirit and began to speak in other tongues, as the Spirit gave them utterance." Note carefully what happened. *They* were filled and began to speak; the Holy Spirit didn't speak; *they* spoke. The Holy Spirit "gave them utterance" or provided the words. The 120 themselves, with their own lips and tongues, did the speaking. The miracle was that the Holy

Spirit furnished them with languages they had never learned.

As you allow the Holy Spirit to furnish you with this new language of praise, remember, you will not be able to understand the language—it will be an unknown tongue to you. But do not let this stop you from speaking. Your responsibility is not to understand but to speak out in faith. At this point, the devil will tempt you and whisper, "You can't do it." But he's a liar! You *can* do it, just as millions of other Christians have. Don't listen to Satan's lies. Ignore him and go ahead and speak.

The Holy Spirit may prompt you to speak in any one of several ways. If you have been praising God in English, you may find your speech becoming difficult, your voice stammering. Yield to this stammering and the new language will form itself easily. Or you may experience the beginning of this "unknown tongue" by having the Holy Spirit insert strange-sounding syllables and words in your mind. Do not dismiss them as mere imagination; you are under the control of the Holy Spirit and the words are from Him. Speak them out in faith, even though you may feel foolish doing so. Peter must have felt foolish walking on water, too.

6. *Keep on speaking in faith.*

Once you have begun to praise God with the new language He has given you, it is important for you to continue to speak until you become completely familiar and comfortable with your new spiritual ability. It may be at this point that your greatest doubts will come. Satan will use your conscious mind, the old mind "of the flesh," to tempt you to reject the whole experience. Just as he tempts you by telling you before you start to speak in tongues that you can't do it, he will also tempt you once you start to speak in tongues by saying, "That's not it! You're just making up sounds and syllables." But just remember he's a liar and don't listen to him. Go ahead and speak and keep on speaking.

Here is the time to profit by Peter's mistake. We have seen how Peter's bold act of faith in stepping over the side of the boat initiated God's miracle. But then we read how Peter took his eyes off Jesus and began staring at the wind-swept water. We can almost hear the words of Satan as he began to taunt Peter about the impossibility of what he was doing. And Peter listened and Peter began to sink. Obviously, his fear came from Satan, for when Jesus reached out and caught him, He chided Peter; "O man of little faith, why did you doubt?" (verse 31).

So it is with your speaking in tongues. You may be so very self-conscious when you first begin to speak, and it may be so different from what you anticipated, that you will wonder if it is all real. *It happens this way with so many people that we can almost reduce it to a law.* You will feel strange and Satan will throw doubts at you. After all, you're traveling in unknown territory. Nothing in your past experience can match it. You're like a baby toddling in a new land. You may even stutter and stammer like a baby at first. Beginning tongues often sound very much like baby talk. But so you stammer, so what? "With stammering lips and another tongue will he speak to this people" (Isaiah 28:11-12 *KJV*). Paul quotes from this passage in Isaiah while discussing tongues (1 Corinthians 14:21). You are in good company!

Don't make the mistake Peter made! The miracle of your speaking in tongues *is* from God, and the doubts which rise to plague you *are* from Satan. Remember Paul's statement, "For if I pray in a tongue, my spirit prays *but my mind is unfruitful*" (1 Corinthians 14:14). In other words, you are not supposed to understand with your intellect what your spirit is praying in tongues. But Satan will use the "unfruitfulness" of your intellect—the fact that you can't make any sense out of the tongues—in an attempt to discredit the miracle which is taking place, just like he used Peter's rationalization about the impossibility of walking on water to cause his faith to falter.

So disregard your doubts; disregard feeling strange; keep your thoughts centered on Jesus as you praise Him in tongues. The more you continue to praise Him, the firmer you will become established in this new spiritual dimension, and the more fluent your praise will become.

We have noted with delight the rich variety of beautiful and worshipful languages in which Spirit-filled friends praise the Lord. But while some people, from the moment of their receiving, demonstrate great fluency in tongues, others seem to speak only a few words or syllables. We've found, however, that a bold faith, coupled with a sense of abandon and willingness to be humbled for Christ's sake, quickly establishes a greater fluency in tongues. Often, the seeming inability to pray freely in tongues is simply a lack of trustful boldness.

Years ago a group of us prayed—seemingly without success—for a young wife to receive the baptism. The following night she returned, at which time she found glorious liberty in praising God in tongues. Then she shared with us how, as we had prayed with her the previous evening, her mind had been filled with strange words and phrases she did not understand. But she had been too shy to speak them aloud. All the next day, as she busied herself with her housework, the Holy Spirit continued to pour such an abundance of unknown words through her thoughts she could think of nothing else.

When we prayed with her a second time, the torrent broke loose, much to her great joy. Many people seem to share a similar reluctance to speak, but the Holy Spirit continues to move in a loving and gracious manner until enough confidence comes to trust Him and to speak out.

The experience of the baptism in the Holy Spirit and speaking in tongues ushers you through a spiritual doorway into all manner of spiritual blessings. Remember, this is not an end, it is a beginning. A whole new realm of spiritual experience lies ahead. Potentially, you have become a powerful and effective witness for Jesus Christ, so don't let Satan rob you of what you have received. Keep your eyes on Jesus, hold fast to the Word of God, practice diligently your new ability to praise God in tongues, and soon you will be firmly grounded in your new life in the Holy Spirit.

"Thanks be to God for his inexpressible gift!" (2 Corinthians 9:15).

CHAPTER 37

I recently received the baptism in the Holy Spirit with speaking in tongues. How do I put my new experience to work?

There is one fact connected with the baptism in the Holy Spirit which we must freely acknowledge: *spiritual power brings problems.* On the surface, one would expect good Christian people to welcome with open arms the witness of other Christians who are eager to share what God has done for them. Unfortunately, this is not always the case. It it inevitable that any Christian who receives the baptism in the Holy Spirit, *and who testifies to what God has done for him*, will face a certain amount of rebuke, rejection and misunderstanding from those with whom he wants most to share the good news. Sobering experience shows that a complacent church may be complacent only as long as no one comes along to challenge its complacency, and an indifferent Christian may remain indifferent only as long as he is free from personal contact with another Christian who is vibrantly alive with the Spirit's power. As Rufus Moseley once said, "No church is so dead that it doesn't resent being told it's dead; and the deader it is, the more it resents it."

The church which lives and ministers "in the flesh," that is, mainly by human effort and planning, and which has not yet experienced spiritual renewal under the power of the Holy Spirit, cannot help but be brought under some measure of conviction and judgment by the appearance of Spirit-filled testimony. We say this, not in condemnation of such a church, but merely in clear realization of the vast gulf which separates "that which is born of the flesh" and "that which is born of the Spirit."

The first problem which you, as one newly baptized in the Holy Spirit, will have to face is how to make an adjustment from the former, perhaps complacent role you played in your church to one which properly reflects your new spiritual life. Some words of caution are in order.

First, remember that receiving the baptism in the Holy Spirit doesn't mean you must become a religious blabbermouth. Don't try to beat people over the head with your experience. There may be a very real temptation to try and share with everyone you meet the wonderful thing which has happened to you. This may be especially true if your baptism was accompanied—as it is for many—by a powerful emotional experience. You "feel so wonderful" you want to tell everyone. But more than one babe in the Holy Spirit has learned from painful experience the truth of Jesus' admonition, "Do not throw your pearls before swine, lest they trample them under foot and turn to attack you" (Matthew 7:6). Don't let the bright glow of a new and powerful experience blind you to the fact that while you may be testifying in a *new* way, with *new* power, about a *new* experience in Christ, most people are listening with the same old ears. And this advice at times proves as pertinent for those of us who have had the baptism in the Holy Spirit for years as for those who have recently received.

For example, I once received a letter from editor

Robert Walker of *Christian Life* magazine containing an editorial report on the first draft of an article I submitted which described the outpouring of the Holy Spirit on the church I was pastoring in Sharon, Pennsylvania. I was surprised and dismayed by two sentences in his letter:

> You do not want to appear cocky, self-righteous or pious, Don. Remember that many people who reject the work of the Holy Spirit are critical of those who claim the infilling of the Spirit because they appear to them to be spiritually proud.

His letter shook me. After all, my article was written to describe the wonderful things Jesus Christ was doing in our church. I certainly did not intend to appear "cocky, self-righteous or pious." Highly miffed, I reread my article. Then I re-read it again as if I were a church member who knew nothing of the charismatic revival, and I quickly saw what my subjective enthusiasm had blinded me to before. I had meant to show, "Look what JESUS CHRIST is doing for us." But in its existing form, the article appeared to boast, "Look what Jesus Christ is doing FOR US." You can be sure the article, as resubmitted to editor Walker, was carefully rewritten.

Secondly, it pays to wait for the Holy Spirit to lead us to the ones to whom we should witness. When we do this, we quickly discover how selective the Holy Spirit can be. Immediately following the baptism in the Holy Spirit, there comes the natural desire to try and share our experience with those closest to us. Occasionally, this works out fine. Other times, it seems to do more harm than good, for our closest friends and relatives often prove to be our severest critics. Even Jesus wasn't believed in his own home town.

Seeking the guidance of the Holy Spirit in the matter of witnessing, we may be surprised to discover Him gently nudging us to keep quiet about our experience when we are among those who have known us the longest and best. The Lord often uses some stranger to make the first contact, and then, at the appropriate time, we are prompted by the Spirit to share our own witness in support of what another has introduced. Jesus' statement often still proves true, "A prophet is not without honor, except in his own country, and among his own kin, and in his own house" (Mark 6:4). At times, I have had to learn the hard way that just because I felt some friend or associate needed my testimony and would welcome it with open arms, it did not necessarily follow that the Holy Spirit shared my enthusiasm.

We need to be on guard, too, against the understandable, but often very unfortunate, impulse to seek out some of the more "spiritually mature" people in our church to share with them our testimony, assuming that their faithfulness in the church and their years of religious activity somehow make them more receptive. Often, just the reverse proves true. For these same devoted and dedicated church members may be so steeped in a certain brand of Christian devotion and service that they simply cannot accept anything new or different. Many of these earnest people—without realizing it of course—are the perfect modern-day counterparts of the Scribes and Pharisees of Jesus' day. For them to accept the fact that vital, supernatural activity of the Holy Spirit working within them should be an integral part of the faith they hold puts too great a strain on their credulity and serves as too severe a judgment on their own ordinary lives. They often find it impossible to admit the validity of any such experience. They are, to quote Rufus Moseley again,

"The hardest nuts to crack and the poorest meat when cracked."

But just as some of the most likely people seem to be the most vehement in their rejection of our witness, so do some of the most unlikely people turn up as candidates for the baptism in the Holy Spirit. We may be sure, when praying about our witness, that the Holy Spirit knows the very people who will be receptive to our testimony and will see to it that they cross our path.

Thirdly, don't be in any big rush to change churches. If your initial attempts to give your witness are met with cool rebuff or even open hostility, you may be strongly tempted to leave your church for some other congregation where you believe people will be more receptive. Go slow! Pray long and hard! Be doubly sure that it is God's will before you make such a move, for if you leave, who will be the witness in your church? Your very difficulties are proof you are needed where you are. The most powerful Christian witness in any congregation may come from the few members who are Spirit-filled, and more than one church has been prayed to life by the earnest intercession of one or two Spirit-filled laymen who resisted the temptation to head for "greener fields" and instead opened the way for revival in their own church by the power of their prayers.

Let your experience of the Holy Spirit draw you into deeper and more loving participation in the life of your church, not only with some charismatic group you may join, but in the church's worship and service as well. Other church members, having heard your testimony, will be waiting—and rightly so—to see the fruit of your experience in your actions. And they will be far more impressed with what you share if the experience leads you into a deeper love for the church and its people, than if they see you deserting the church to start off on some tangent of your own.

For the minister receiving the baptism in the Holy Spirit, things may prove somewhat more difficult, depending on the stand of his particular denomination concerning the charismatic revival. It is true that some ministers, on making public their testimony, have been forced to resign. In some cases this appears inevitable. Perhaps some churches can only be made aware of what God is doing in our day through this kind of open break. But we must also honestly admit to situations where, if the minister had been a little less precipitous, if he had been just a little more loving and a little more patient, his testimony would have been accepted by some and perhaps tolerated by all.

Of course, we recognize that every situation must be judged on its own merits, and there is little way of predicting how the Holy Spirit will move and what will be the reaction to His moving in every case. But one thing seems clear; if we are patient, faithful and trusting, God will open a way for our testimony, either where we presently are, or in some situation to which He will lead us.

A fourth word of advice is: *be careful, but be a witness!* At the opposite end of being too bold and premature in witnessing, there is the equal, if not greater, danger of silencing our witness. I am especially sensitive to this sin, not only because I was personally guilty of it (the result being several years of relatively fruitless ministry), but also because of the increasing number of Christians who have received the baptism in the Holy Spirit but are doing nothing with it.

Surely, we are not mistaken in believing that God expects every Spirit-filled Christian to witness. Even if it seems impossible in your own-church, there are other avenues open where your witness may be shared and your experience deepened. Most of us live near some town or city where there is a Full Gospel Business Men's Fellowship International chapter whose monthly meetings can serve as a vital source of Spirit-filled fellowship. In every town of any size, there is at least one charismatic prayer group—usually interdenominational—meeting in a home or church. Such groups not only offer inspiration and fellowship, they also help keep us "aglow with the Spirit," giving us confidence to speak the quiet word of witness where we work or in our own church and among our friends and neighbors. These charismatic groups and FGBMFI chapters are also ideal for introducing your friends to the baptism in the Holy Spirit without getting involved in denominationalism or the question of "church membership," for such groups are completely non-denominational.

A fifth, and perhaps most important point to remember in our discussion of the problems connected with witnessing is this: *the primary purpose of our witnessing is to lift up and glorify Jesus Christ* and not any particular experience. Because of the rather spectacular nature of the baptism in the Holy Spirit and because much of the criticism and questions about the baptism center on the supernatural gifts accompanying it, especially speaking in tongues, there comes a temptation to overstress the gifts rather than to give glory to the Giver; to defend the baptism rather than to exalt the Baptizer. Look again at Jesus' promise in Acts 1:8, "Ye shall receive power, after that the Holy Ghost is come upon you: and ye shall be *witnesses unto me...*" *(KJV).* Note that Jesus said, "witnesses unto me," not "witnesses unto the baptism in the Holy Spirit."

This truth is pointed out another time in John 16:14. "He (the Holy Spirit) will glorify me, for he will take what is mine and declare it to you." The Holy Spirit brings power to witness, but our witness is not to the baptism in the Holy Spirit or to spiritual gifts, but to Jesus Christ. Perhaps a blunt statement for the sake of emphasis is in order here. ANY TESTIMONY CONCERNING THE BAPTISM IN THE HOLY SPIRIT WHICH OMITS GLORIFYING JESUS CHRIST AS SAVIOR AND BAPTIZER IS INCOMPLETE.

Reverend David Wilkerson, author of *The Cross and The Switchblade*, and founder of Teen Challenge in Brooklyn, New York, once shared with me an interesting experience which illustrates the point we are making here. A young minister came to visit Teen Challenge because he had been impressed at what he had heard concerning the baptism in the Holy Spirit and its dramatic effects on the lives of former addicts.

"He had no firsthand knowledge of the baptism in the Holy Spirit," David said, "so several of us spent about an hour in my office with him, explaining the experience; how it gave power, how it introduced the Christian to the supernatural experience of speaking in tongues, and how dramatic deliverance from illness and addiction often took place by the Holy Spirit's power.

"The young minister listened very attentively until we were through," David continued, "and then made a single, devastating comment. He said, 'But Reverend Wilkerson, I thought the Holy Spirit was given to glorify Jesus Christ. And although I have sat here for an hour listening to you and your staff members relate all the wonderful things the Holy Spirit is doing, not one of you mentioned the name of our Lord Jesus even once.'

"The Lord used that young man to humble us all,"

David concluded, "and to impress upon us once again that the primary purpose of the Holy Spirit in our lives is to glorify the Lord Jesus Christ."

Finally, a sixth word of caution: the Spirit-filled life needs nurture. We must frankly admit there are some who, after being baptized by Jesus in the Holy Spirit, decide to ignore Spirit-filled fellowship. The results are often tragic. The baptism in the Holy Spirit is a *crisis* experience and must be followed by the *continuing* experience of walking daily in the Spirit. It is difficult, if not impossible, to grow spiritually apart from Christian fellowship. We need to be continually "refilled" or recharged in the dynamic fellowship which comes from the Spirit-filled body of believers. For this reason, we urge everyone coming into the baptism in the Holy Spirit to link himself up to some charismatic fellowship, somewhere.

Even after the first Pentecost, Jesus' disciples frequently met together in prayer-filled fellowship where the Holy Spirit could bless and strengthen them. In the fourth chapter of Acts, we find such an occasion with the disciples gathered together, praying for strength to witness and asking God to perform miracles to confirm their ministry. Verse 31 tells how God answered their prayer.

> And when they had prayed, the place in which they gathered together was shaken; and they were all filled with the Holy Spirit and spoke the word of God with boldness.

Someone once asked the great Dwight L. Moody why he testified to having received many "infillings" of the

Holy Spirit. Moody's classic reply was, "I leak." And so do we all!

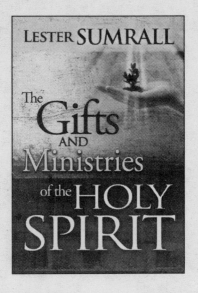

The Gifts and Ministries of the Holy Spirit
Lester Sumrall

The gifts of the Spirit can destroy any force the devil might use against Christians. You are a candidate to receive the Holy Spirit gifts of revelation, power, and inspiration. They will function anywhere—right where you are now! Dr. Lester Sumrall explores many relevant aspects of *The Gifts and Ministries of the Holy Spirit* including the weapons of our warfare, how you can receive the gifts, the devil's counterfeit, and the purpose of ministry gifts. Discover how you can be included in the great outpouring of God's Spirit!

ISBN: 0-88368-652-X • Trade • 272 pages

www.whitakerhouse.com

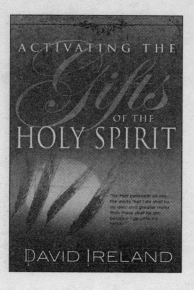

Activating the Gifts of the Holy Spirit
David Ireland

God has destined you to move in the gifts of the
Spirit with ease and ability. He has planned that
the gifts become evident in every area of your
life. David Ireland provides practical lessons on
entering into and operating in the realm of the
supernatural, so that you can be miraculously
used by God to minister to others. Discover
how you can experience spiritual power in
your everyday walk with God.

ISBN: 0-88368-484-5 • Trade • 192 pages

www.whitakerhouse.com

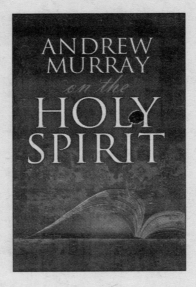

Andrew Murray on the Holy Spirit
Andrew Murray

Sent by the Father, the Holy Spirit is your Comforter
when you are worried or afraid, your Strength when you
are weak, your Safety when you are in danger, and your
Peace in the midst of confusion. Beloved author Andrew
Murray explores the divine life that is meant for every
child of God. Discover how you can receive the Holy
Spirit, have direct communication with God, obtain all that
God has for you, overcome Satan's power, and inherit the
promises of the Bible. A dynamic, joyful life that is filled
with the presence of the Holy Spirit can be yours today!

ISBN: 0-88368-846-8 • Trade • 208 pages

WHITAKER HOUSE
www.whitakerhouse.com

The Presence and Work of the Holy Spirit
R. A. Torrey

Discover the importance of the presence of the Holy Spirit in the believer's life! R. A. Torrey also shows how to receive God's favor and blessings, the way the Holy Spirit imparts life to the spiritually dead, and our need to follow the Holy Spirit's guidance. These eternal issues—and many more—are covered in this in-depth examination of who the Holy Spirit is and His work in our lives. Followers of Christ, as well as those searching, will be permanently transformed as God's divine power flows through their hearts.

ISBN: 0-88368-177-3 • Trade • 256 pages

WHITAKER
HOUSE
www.whitakerhouse.com

Smith Wigglesworth on Spiritual Gifts
Smith Wigglesworth

As Smith Wigglesworth explains the role and function of
spiritual gifts, he provides important spiritual safeguards
for the proper exercise of these manifestations of the
Holy Spirit. Through his simple yet profound words,
you will find out how to receive God's healing and
discernment, minister to others in Christ's love, and
operate in the gifts of the Spirit wisely. You can be
the instrument God uses to transmit His love and
miracles to a hurting, needy world.

ISBN: 0-88368-533-7 • Trade • 224 pages

www.whitakerhouse.com

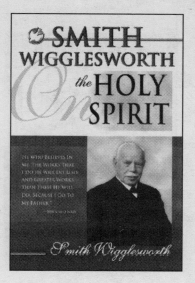

Smith Wigglesworth on the Holy Spirit
Smith Wigglesworth

You can be so filled with the Holy Spirit that you will know you are in the presence of God. Christ's love, power, and joy will flow through you to others, bringing salvation, healing, and miracles, just as they did through Smith Wigglesworth. Learn how the fullness of the Holy Spirit can be yours. God will work mightily in you by the power of His Spirit so that you can overcome all the schemes of Satan and do greater works for His kingdom.

ISBN: 0-88368-544-2 • Trade • 224 pages

The Holy Spirit in You
Derek Prince

Derek Prince clearly explains the ways of the Holy Spirit and how He works in the lives of Christians. Discover how you can, through the power of the Holy Spirit, experience the continual presence of Jesus, become bold a witness for Christ, pray according to God's will, and receive physical and emotional healing. As you understand and receive the active presence of the Spirit in your life, you will gain new power and grace for living.

ISBN: 0-88368-961-8 • Trade • 112 pages

www.whitakerhouse.com